General editor: Graham Handley

Brodie's Notes on William Shakespeare's
# The Tempest

T. W. Smith BA
Former English Master, Barrow and Teignmouth Grammar Schools

MACMILLAN

© Macmillan Press Ltd 1991

All rights reserved. No reproduction, copy or transmission of
this publication may be made without written permission.

No paragraph of this publication may be reproduced, copied or
transmitted save with written permission or in accordance with
the provisions of the Copyright, Designs and Patents Act 1988,
or under the terms of any licence permitting limited copying
issued by the Copyright Licensing Agency, 90 Tottenham Court
Road, London W1P 9HE.

Any person who does any unauthorised act in relation to this
publication may be liable to criminal prosecution and civil
claims for damages.

First published by James Brodie Ltd
This revised edition first published 1990
by Pan Books Ltd

Published 1992 by
MACMILLAN PRESS LTD
Houndmills, Basingstoke, Hampshire RG21 6XS
and London
Companies and representatives
throughout the world

ISBN 0-333-58177-6

8   7   6   5   4   3   2
01  00  99  98  97  96  95

Printed in Great Britain by
Cox and Wyman Ltd, Reading, Berks

# Contents

**Preface by the general editor**  5

**Shakespeare and the Elizabethan playhouse**  7

**Literary terms used in these notes**  11

**The play**
Plot  13
Sources  15
Treatment  16
Text and date  18

**Scene summaries, critical commentary, textual notes and revision questions**
Act I  20
Act II  34
Act III  42
Act IV  50
Act V  57

**Shakespeare's art in *The Tempest***

**Introduction**  66

**Structure, themes, setting**  69

**The characters**
Prospero 75, Miranda 77, Ferdinand 77, Ariel 78, Caliban 80, Alonso, Antonio, Sebastian 82, Gonzalo 83, Stephano and Trinculo 84

**Style**
Introduction, Verse, Use of prose  86

**General questions and sample answer in note form**  90

**Further reading**  93

Line references in these Notes are to the
*Arden Shakespeare: The Tempest*,
but as references are also given to particular acts
and scenes, the Notes may be used with any
edition of the play.

# Preface

This student revision aid is based on the principle that in any close examination of Shakespeare's plays 'the text's the thing'. Seeing a performance, or listening to a tape or record of a performance, is essential and is in itself a valuable and stimulating experience in understanding and appreciation. However, a real evaluation of Shakespeare's greatness, of his universality and of the nature of his literary and dramatic art, can only be achieved by constant application to the texts of the plays themselves. These revised editions of Brodie's Notes are intended to supplement that process through detailed critical commentary.

The first aim of each book is to fix the whole play in the reader's mind by providing a concise summary of the plot, relating it back, where appropriate, to its source or sources. Subsequently the book provides a summary of each scene, followed by *critical comments*. These may convey its importance in the dramatic structure of the play, creation of atmosphere, indication of character development, significance of figurative language etc, and they will also explain or paraphrase difficult words or phrases and identify meaningful references. At the end of each act revision questions are set to test the student's specific and broad understanding and appreciation of the play.

An extended critical commentary follows this scene by scene analysis. This embraces such major elements as characterization, imagery, the use of blank verse and prose, soliloquies and other aspects of the play which the editor considers need close attention. The paramount aim is to send the reader back to the text. The book concludes with a series of revision questions which require a detailed knowledge of the play; the first of these has notes by the editor of what *might* be included in a written answer. The intention is to stimulate and to guide; the whole emphasis of this commentary is to encourage the student's *involvement* in the play, to develop disciplined critical responses and thus promote personal enrichment through the imaginative experience of our greatest writer.

**Graham Handley**

# Shakespeare and the Elizabethan playhouse

William Shakespeare was born in Stratford-upon-Avon in 1564, and there are reasons to suppose that he came from a relatively prosperous family. He was probably educated at Stratford Grammar School and, at the age of eighteen, married Anne Hathaway, who was twenty-six. They had three children, a girl born shortly after their marriage, followed by twins in 1585 (the boy died in 1596). It seems likely that Shakespeare left for London shortly after a company of visiting players had visited Stratford in 1585, for by 1592 – according to the jealous testimony of one of his fellow-writers Robert Greene – he was certainly making his way both as actor and dramatist. The theatres were closed because of the plague in 1593; when they reopened Shakespeare worked with the Lord Chamberlain's men, later the King's Men, and became a shareholder in each of the two theatres with which he was most closely associated, the Globe and the Blackfriars. He later purchased New Place, a considerable property in his home town of Stratford, to which he retired in 1611; there he entertained his great contemporary Ben Jonson (1572–1637) and the poet Michael Drayton (1563–1631). An astute businessman, Shakespeare lived comfortably in the town until his death in 1616.

This is a very brief outline of the life of our greatest writer, for little more can be said of him with certainty, though the plays – and poems – are living witness to the wisdom, humanity and many-faceted nature of the man. He was both popular and successful as a dramatist, perhaps less so as an actor. He probably began work as a dramatist in the late 1580s, by collaborating with other playwrights and adapting old plays, and by 1598 Francis Meres was paying tribute to his excellence in both comedy and tragedy. His first original play was probably *Love's Labour's Lost* (1590) and while the theatres were closed during the plague he wrote his narrative poems *Venus and Adonis* (1593) and *The Rape of Lucrece* (1594). The sonnets were almost certainly written in the 1590s though not published until 1609; the first 126 seem to be addressed to a young man who was his friend and patron, while the rest are concerned with the 'dark lady'.

The dating of Shakespeare's plays has exercised scholars ever since the publication of the First Folio (1623), which listed them as comedies, histories and tragedies. It seems more important to look at them chronologically as far as possible, in order to trace Shakespeare's considerable development as a dramatist. The first period, say to the middle of the 1590s, included such plays as *Love's Labour's Lost*, *The Comedy of Errors*, *Richard III*, *The Taming of the Shrew*, *Romeo and Juliet* and *Richard II*. These early plays embrace the categories listed in the First Folio, so that Shakespeare the craftsman is evident in his capacity for variety of subject and treatment. The next phase includes *A Midsummer's Night's Dream*, *The Merchant of Venice*, *Henry IV Parts 1* and *2*, *Henry V* and *Much Ado About Nothing*, as well as *Julius Caesar*, *As You Like It* and *Twelfth Night*. These are followed, in the early years of the 17th century, by his great tragic period: *Hamlet*, *Othello*, *King Lear* and *Macbeth*, with *Antony and Cleopatra* and *Coriolanus* belonging to 1607–09. The final phase embraces the romances (1610–13), *Cymbeline*, *The Tempest* and *The Winter's Tale* and the historical play *Henry VIII*.

Each of these revision aids will place the individual text under examination in the chronology of the remarkable dramatic output that spanned twenty years from the early 1590s to about 1613. The practical theatre for which Shakespeare wrote and acted derived from the inn courtyards in which performances had taken place, the few playhouses in his day being modelled on their structure. They were circular or hexagonal in shape, allowing from the balconies and boxes around the walls full view of the stage. This large stage, which had no scenery, jutted out into the pit, the most extensive part of the theatre, where the poorer people – the 'groundlings' – stood. There was no roof (though the Blackfriars, used from 1608 onwards, was an indoor theatre) and thus bad weather meant no performance. Certain plays were acted at court, and these private performances normally marked some special occasion. Costumes, often rich ones, were used, and music was a common feature, with musicians on or under the stage; this sometimes had additional features, for example a trapdoor to facilitate the entry of a ghost. Women were barred by law from appearing on stage, and all female parts were played by boy actors; this undoubtedly explains the many instances in Shakespeare where a woman has to conceal her identity by disguising

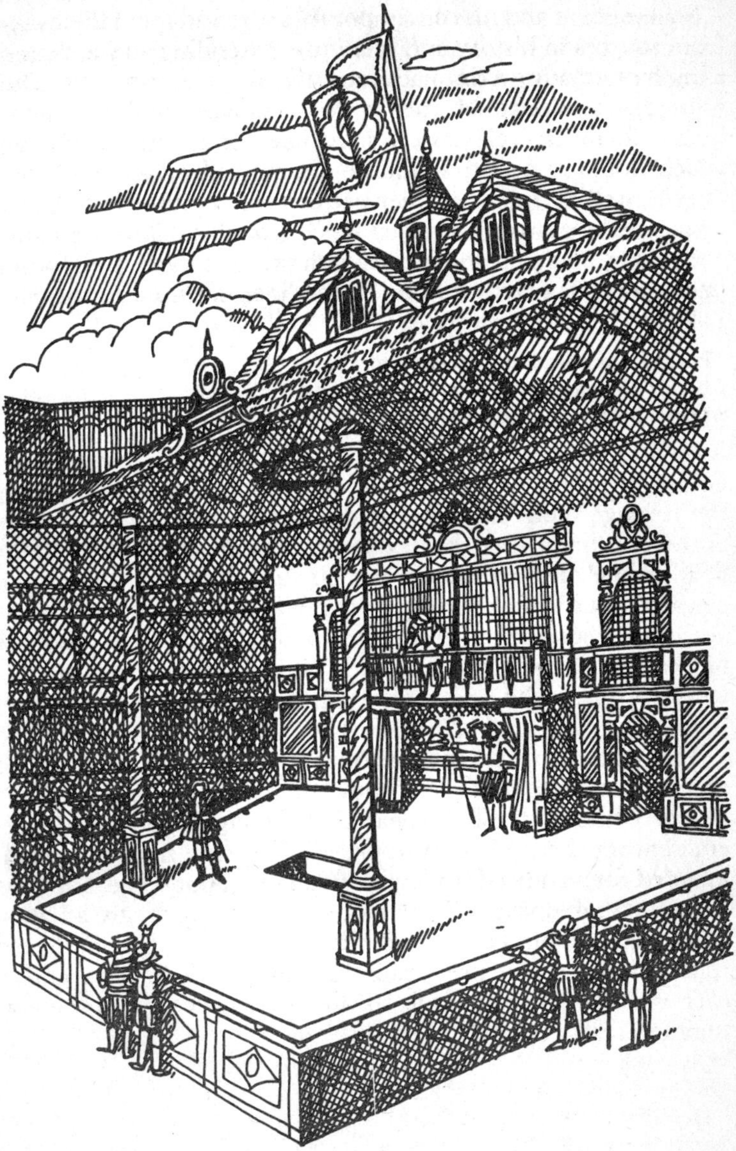

herself as a man, e.g. Rosalind in *As You Like It*, Viola in *Twelfth Night*.

Shakespeare and his contemporaries often adapted their plays from sources in history and literature, extending an incident or a myth or creating a dramatic narrative from known facts. They were always aware of their own audiences, and frequently included topical references, sometimes of a satirical flavour, which would appeal to – and be understood by – the groundlings as well as their wealthier patrons who occupied the boxes. Shakespeare obviously learned much from his fellow dramatists and actors, being on good terms with many of them. Ben Jonson paid generous tribute to him in the lines prefaced to the First Folio of Shakespeare's plays:

Thou art a monument without a tomb,
And art alive still, while thy book doth live
And we have wits to read, and praise to give.

Among his contemporaries were Thomas Kyd (1558–94) and Christopher Marlowe (1564–93). Kyd wrote *The Spanish Tragedy*, the revenge motif here foreshadowing the much more sophisticated treatment evident in *Hamlet*, while Marlowe evolved the 'mighty line' of blank verse, a combination of natural speech and elevated poetry. The quality and variety of Shakespeare's blank verse owes something to the innovatory brilliance of Marlowe but carries the stamp of individuality, richness of association, technical virtuosity and, above all, the genius of imaginative power.

The texts of Shakespeare's plays are still rich sources for scholars, and the editors of these revision aids have used the Arden editions of Shakespeare, which are regarded as preeminent for their scholarly approach. They are strongly recommended for advanced students, but other editions, like The New Penguin Shakespeare, The New Swan, The Signet, are all good annotated editions currently available. A reading list of selected reliable works on the play being studied is provided at the end of each commentary and students are advised to turn to these as their interest in the play deepens.

# Literary terms used in these notes

**Simile** The discovery of a striking resemblance between two objects, attitudes or actions different otherwise from each other, introduced by 'like' or 'as'. The second, which should be familiar, throws new and often picturesque light on the first. Examples of this and other poetic imagery are scarce in the play.
They'll take suggestion *as a cat laps milk* (II,1,283).
                          their great guilt,
*Like poison given to work a great time after,*
Now 'gins to bite the spirits (III,3,105–6).
His tears runs down his beard, *like winter's drops*
*From eaves of reeds* (V,1,16–17).
Many expressions beginning with 'like' or 'as' are merely comparisons:
Dew-lapp'd like bulls (III,3,45).
As fast as mill-wheels strike (I,2,281).

**Metaphor** Essentially this is a condensed simile, not introduced by 'like' or 'as'.
The ivy which had hid my princely trunk (I,2,86).
The fringed curtains of thine eye advance (I,2,411).
The jewel in my dower (my modesty, III,1,54).
There is a double metaphor in the pun on 'key' – to a door and to a musical instrument – in I,2,83–5.

**Personification** Treating inanimate objects or abstract ideas as persons, indicated usually but not necessarily by a capital letter:
You are three men of sin, whom Destiny . . .
Hath caus'd to belch up you; (III,3,53–6).
my trust . . . did beget of him/A falsehood (I,2,93–5).
To th'shore, that o'er his (i.e. its) wave-worn basis bowed,
As stooping to relieve him (II,1,116–7).
                        *barren* hate,
*Sour-ey'd* disdain and discord shall *bestrew*
The union of your bed with weeds (IV, 1, 19–21)
Here the personification is due to the epithets and the action of strewing; the latter makes the number of evil spirits three.

**Allusion** The special mention, usually brief, of a person, place or event, directly by name or indirectly by some quality, often to make a comparison, complimentary or otherwise. Allusions to mythical characters were frequent in poetry from the Renaissance onwards:
Antonio compares Gonzalo to the 'parish visitor' (II,1,11); Caliban is made to refer to the familiar Bible incident in which Jael slew Sisera with a nail in the head (III, 2, 60).

**Antithesis** The balancing of two opposite ideas or expressions in the same phrase or sentence.

**Apostrophe** Turning aside to address a god, an abstraction or a person as if present. Also the direct address, blunt or appealing (V, 1, 62–79).

**Archaism** Use of a word or expression that is obsolete, but employed for poetic effect or to create an impression of a past age. A large proportion of Shapespeare's vocabulary is archaic, like 'flats' for swamps in II, 2, 2.

**Chiasmus** In the second part the order of words in the first part is reversed: 'All hail, great master! grave sir, hail!' (I, 2, 189).

**Climax** The arrangement of three or more objects in ascending order of importance (the Greek word means a 'ladder'); now usually misapplied to the highest point of any development. Act IV, Scene 1, 152–4 forms a true climax.

**Conceit** A highly artificial figure of speech (popular in Elizabethan days). See Ferdinand's profession of pure love in IV, 1, 55–6.

**Dramatic irony** This occurs when a character in a play makes a remark showing he is unaware of a fact known to the audience. For example, Alonso's wish that the two 'lost' children could have been married, V, 1, 149–50.

**Epithet** A descriptive adjective giving the characteristic quality of someone or something: the 'mutinous' winds (V, 1, 42).

**Hyperbole** Exaggeration for the sake of emphasis: 'Ten leagues beyond man's life' (II, 1, 242).

**Inversion** Another emphatic device (often used in rhetoric) in which an object precedes the verb or the subject comes last: 'their labour Delight in them sets off' (III, 1, 1–2). Here the object precedes the subject.

**Irony** Saying the opposite of what is meant, usually for sarcastic effect: 'we prosper well in our return', referring to the shipwreck (II, 1, 69).

**Oxymoron** Two words expressing opposing ideas are used together: 'loving wrong' (I, 2, 151).

**Pathetic Fallacy** Personal feelings are attributed to natural features: 'loving wrong', i.e. the winds, out of love for us, did us the least injury.

**Periphrasis** Using a descriptive definition instead of the object itself for special effect (roundabout phraseology): acorn-cups become 'husks Wherein the acorn cradled' (I, 2, 466–7).

**Soliloquy** A speech uttered by a character when alone on the stage, as if to himself, but really for the benefit of the audience. Examples are by Prospero (V, 1, 33–57), Ferdinand (III, 1, 1–14) and Caliban (II, 2, 1–14).

**Tautology** Unnecessary repetition, though sometimes used rhetorically: 'all foison, all abundance' (II, 1, 159).

# The play

**Plot**

Alonso, King of Naples, is returning by sea from the marriage of his daughter Claribel to the King of Tunis when his fleet is overtaken by a violent storm. The King's ship is separated from the others and driven towards the coast of an island. In spite of the desperate efforts of the crew, the ship strikes the rocks, and the terrified passengers leap overboard.

The rest of the action takes place on the island. Prospero, formerly Duke of Milan, explains to his daughter Miranda how, twelve years before, he lost his dukedom through a conspiracy between his brother Antonio and King Alonso. A Neapolitan named Gonzalo was charged with abandoning him and his infant daughter at sea in a leaky boat, but out of compassion this Gonzalo provided him with food, clothes, and those books he most valued. Arriving at the island he found a misshapen savage in possession, the offspring of a witch banished there from Algiers. This Caliban he sought to educate, but the experiment was a failure and the monster became the household drudge. Prospero's magic also released a spirit, Ariel, from confinement in a pine-tree, on condition that he obeyed Prospero's commands in all the elements of earth, sea and air. Ariel's last task before regaining complete freedom is the management of the storm, preservation from harm of the vessel and those on board, and the control of the movements of the various individuals who have reached land.

By his airy music Ariel lures the King's son Ferdinand from the shore to Prospero's cell, where the young prince takes Miranda for the goddess of the place, while she in turn is fascinated by this first visitor from the outside world. Prospero, who sees in the growing love of the young couple the future union of Naples and Milan, is determined to strengthen the bond by making the path of true love anything but smooth. Ferdinand is made prisoner and condemned to carry logs.

Meanwhile, miraculously saved from drowning, Alonso laments the loss of his son. Old Gonzalo seeks to cheer him with philosophy, but his attempts only irritate the moody monarch and are scoffed at by Antonio and the King's brother Sebastian. While the rest are deep in a sleep induced by Ariel, Antonio and Sebastian are about to slay the King and Gonzalo, when the latter is awakened by Ariel. The would-be assassins excuse their drawn swords by declaring that they had heard lions. The party then sets off to search for Ferdinand.

Caliban, in constant terror of being hurt by Prospero's spirits, encounters Trinculo the jester and Stephano the butler and, his tongue loosened by the liquor so freely dispensed by Stephano from a salvaged wine-keg, swears to make him master of the island once Prospero is killed. The drunken trio start for the magician's cell but, intercepted by Ariel, are lured through briars and gorse and finally left up to their necks in a stagnant pool.

Another kind of torment awaits the royal party. Spirits lay a banquet before their hungry eyes only for Ariel to appear in the guise of a harpy and lecture them on the wrong done to the former Duke of Milan, after which the food vanishes. The three 'men of sin', convinced that they have to deal with fiends, rush frantically off to grapple with the unknown.

Ferdinand's penance having cemented the love of the young people, Prospero gives them his blessing and entertains them with a typical wedding masque. Towards the end, Prospero suddenly remembers Caliban's scheme (of which Ariel has already informed him), dismisses the others and summons Ariel – who has, as usual, obeyed his instructions 'to the syllable'. Together they watch Stephano and Trinculo, in spite of Caliban's warning, fall for the glittering raiment hung up as bait; then they drive the butler and jester away, setting spirits in the shape of hounds upon them.

In the last Act Prospero's whole scheme for bringing home the crime of his banishment to the malefactors reaches its culmination. Alonso resigns Prospero's dukedom and asks pardon for the wrongs he has done him, and Prospero's 'art', having fulfilled its purpose, is laid aside for ever.

Held within a charmed circle, the courtiers behold Prospero arrayed once more as Duke of Milan. Reconciliation is followed by a final 'conceit' – the discovery of the King's lost son in the company of the Duke's 'lost' daughter. The blasphemous boatswain, born to be hanged, brings news that the ship is in good trim for the journey back to Italy. The comic trio are brought in for the general amusement, and Caliban sees 'King' Stephano in his proper perspective.

Finally, after inviting his guests into his cell for the night, Prospero speaks of spending his old age in Milan, <u>and, in an epilogue, renounces his magician's spell and appeals to the audience to release him from *their* spell by giving him a good clap.</u>

## Sources

Nearly all Shakespeare's plots can be traced, with varying degrees of certainty, to their originals. *The Tempest* is one of the exceptions, though there has been some interesting guesswork. It was Shakespeare's custom to use material at hand, and a pamphlet which appeared in 1610, *A Discovery of the Bermudas, otherwise called the Ile of Divels*, by Silvester Jourdan, contains the following passage:

For the Ilandes of the Bermudas, as every man knoweth that hath heard or read of them, were never inhabited by any Christian or Heathen people, but ever esteemed and reputed a most prodigious and inchanted place, affording nothing but gusts, stormes and foule weather; which made every Navigator and Mariner to avoide them ... Yet did we finde there the ayre so temperate and the Country so abundantly fruitful of all fit necessaries for the sustentation and preservation of mans life ... that we were there for the space of nine months ... well refreshed.

This is one of several accounts of the adventures that befell an expedition of colonists from London to Virginia. The flagship, carrying the Admiral, Sir George Somers, was separated from the other seven ships by a storm. His ship was leaking badly when the Admiral spied land, and, though the Bermudas had an evil reputation, it was a case of 'any port in a storm'. A high tide lodged the ship between two rocks, and all escaped to the shore, where they found the climate pleasant and land fruitful. Nine months later, having built two vessels they continued their way to Virginia. Later some of the seamen arrived in London and aroused great public interest by their story.

Resemblances have also been noted to a German play, *Die Schöne Sidea* by Jacob Ayrer, which contained a magician; his only daughter, who falls in love with a log-carrying prisoner; and an attendant spirit. English players had been to Nuremberg in 1604, and from them Shakespeare may have borrowed some

16 The Tempest

ideas, or both plays may well have a common origin yet to be discovered, as well as some unknown chronicle of the union of the houses of Naples and Milan.

Besides the features or incidents for which such parallels have been suggested, there are passages in which the imagery seems to be heavily indebted to Shakespeare's reading of particular works. This is very evident from a comparison, for example, of Gonzalo's 'commonwealth' with a relevant piece in Florio's translation of Montaigne's *Essais* (see note on II,1,143) or of Prospero's soliloquy with lines in Golding's translation of Ovid's *Metamorphoses* (see note V,1,35).

## Treatment

Out of the elaborate details of contemporary pamphlets circulated by returned explorers and the small change of random tales in London taverns, Shakespeare gained sufficient material to create an illusion of maritime nature at its worst, with strong winds stirring up mountainous billows and piling a helpless vessel onto rocks. Suddenly we are made to realize that the storm itself (more awe-inspiring when designated a 'tempest' – the word, now verging on the archaic, almost belongs to the play) is a product of human genius operating through elemental spirits to fulfil the twin 'projects' of (1) punishing with remorse and mistaken sorrow one wrongdoer, and (2) bringing about the meeting of two young people of some dynastic importance (a topic suited to entertain the guests at a royal marriage).

It all 'comes to a head' in the short space of twenty-four hours and the confined space of a rocky islet, where the storm has subsided and there is little room for action except the drawing of a sword or the thrust of a dagger; only the stage productions of the spirit world interrupt the flow of argument and admonition. The dialogue in fact goes through the whole gamut of human intercourse: grieving, praising, praying, swearing, entreating, sneering, welcoming, condemning. There is constant contrast – between youth and age, loyalty and treachery, delicacy of sentiment and coarseness of vulgar impulse.

The play is a 'romance', its theme is forgiveness, and its plot is diversified by the comic misfortunes of two Shakespearian characters who escape drowning only to plunge up to their ears in a filthy pond. Diversified, too, by two masque-like performances: (1) a 'banquet' conjured out of thin air to be then spirited away while a Harpy (visible only to the audience) pronounces judgment on the 'men of sin', and (2) a parade of classical goddesses assembled to bless the betrothal of the only woman in the play to her prince.

Masques, originating in Italy, became popular in England under James I. Ben Jonson, friend of Shakespeare, with forty to his credit, is their chief representative in our literature. Spectacular, with sketchy plots full of allegory and symbols, they were designed for performance by aristocratic amateurs on special occasions, helped out by professionals who would be responsible for the more fantastic anti-masques (grotesque appearance and gestures). Jacobean money was typically lavished on scenery, costumes and musical accompaniment.

Prospero's island made a good setting, the effects of elaborate stage devices being ascribed to the prevailing enchantment, in contrast to the more serious business of contemporary 'plantation', exposed to human deceit and trickery. Compare the sober jottings of Sir Francis Bacon (long thought by some to be the real author of Shakespeare's plays) in his severely practical Essay 'Plantations':

The People wherewith you Plant ought to be Gardners, Ploughmen, Labourers, Smiths, Carpenters, Ioyners, Fisher-men, Fowlers, with some few Apothecaries, Surgeons, Cookes, and Bakers. On a country of Plantation, first looke about, what kinde of Victuall the Countrie yeelds of it selfe to Hand: As Chestnuts, Wallnuts, Pine-Apples, Olives, Dates, Plummes, Cherries, Wilde-Hony, and the like; and make use of them ... Wood commonly aboundeth but too much; And therefore, Timber is fit to be one (i.e. a profitable commodity).

Ferdinand's stint was reckoned by him in thousands of logs; it is not clear whether these were needed as goods for sale, timber for hut construction, fuel in a Mediterranean winter or just a drill-ground fatigue!

The sea in all its moods and the winds that play upon it have supplied Shakespeare with figures and analogies throughout his works; in the last of the dramas it has become a presence in itself, ready to drown and break to pieces. Elsewhere we have seaports, seamen, sea-borne commerce, accounts of wrecks, risky voyages etc. Here the sea surrounds a tiny island, leagues from any mainland, a sanctuary for exiles, for Sycorax from Algiers, for Prospero from Milan. Its economy is as mysterious as the sea, all things needed being provided by a wave of the wand. Two questions propose themselves: (1) Why did the magician not turn his 'cell' into a palazzo? (2) How did Gonzalo know Prospero was a chess-player?

## Text and date

Few readers of Shakespeare realize the difficulties that scholars have had to overcome in order to establish accurate texts of the plays. The First Folio contained thirty-six plays. Other collected editions or Folios were published later in the seventeenth century, the Third and Fourth Folios containing seven additional plays, none of which, with the exception of *Pericles*, is now thought to be by Shakespeare. Sixteen of the plays had already been published separately as Quartos before 1623, and in the case of some plays, for example, *Hamlet*, more than one Quarto edition exists. Some of these Quartos are almost word for word the same as the texts in the First Folio and were possibly set up from Shakespeare's own manuscript or at least from accurate theatre copies; but others are shortened, inferior versions, possibly 'pirated' editions published by some unauthorized person who had access to theatre copies or parts of them, or who had taken down the plays in shorthand while they were being performed. It is thought that the texts of the First Folio were set up from the good Quartos and from good theatre copies. But these texts must all be compared, printers' mistakes and other interference traced, before a reliable text can be arrived at.

The first editor to attempt the problem of the text was Nicholas Rowe (1674–1718), who also divided most of the plays into acts and scenes, supplied place-names of the location of each scene, indications of entrances and exits and a list of dramatis personae, which are absent from many of the texts in the Quarto and Folio editions. In *The Tempest*, however, all the acts and scenes are marked. The play (classed as a comedy) is the first play of the Folio, and is one of a few plays therein with a list of the characters, and the only play with the scene of the action specifically stated – 'an un-inhabited Island', which seems to show that two of the actors who took part in *The Tempest*, at all events, did not consider Caliban as a human being. The divisions into acts and scenes are convenient for reference (like the divisions of the books of the Bible into chapters and verses) but have no important use in Shakespearian study. They were fitted for the stage of his time, but were unnecessary on Shakespeare's stage, where the minimum of scenery was used.

*The Tempest* was one of the plays performed in February 1613 at the court of James I during the celebrations in honour of the betrothal of his daughter Elizabeth to the German Prince Frederick, Elector Palatine. It is possible that for this occasion the play in its original form was cut in order to include the masque in Act IV and to restrict the duration of the performance. This would also explain the length of Act 1, Scene 2, in which earlier scenes may have been summarized, and account for the fragmentary characters of Adrian and Francisco.

*Date* The likeliest year of composition lies between 1610, when news reached London of the ill-fated expedition of Sir George Somers, and the dynastically important wedding of 1613 (from which came our Hanoverian sovereigns). There are interesting parallels with James's hostility to witchcraft, the sad death of his elder son Henry in 1612, and the departure overseas of his daughter.

# Scene summaries, critical commentary, textual notes and revision questions

### Act I Scene 1

The ship carrying a King and his court is being driven onto the rocks by a violent storm. The passengers, partly in terror, partly indignant at the boatswain's lack of respect, keep coming on deck and getting in the way of the crew. Though in the darkness and confusion the characters cannot yet be identified, three of the royal suite speak already 'in character': one old man finds comfort in the belief that the boatswain, with the look of a gallows-bird, was born to be hanged, and not drowned; the two future villains abuse the harassed seamen and accuse them of responsibility for the wreck.

Amid the howls of the passengers below and the despairing cries of the helpless mariners, the ship is split on the rocks. Like a shaft of light relief in the prevailing gloom the old man offers a whole ocean for one acre of the poorest soil on land.

### *Commentary*

This opening scene is noteworthy in the following ways:
1 Its nautical bustle and human distress provide a realistic background to the unreal incidents in the play and the supernatural character of the island.
2 It presents the full fury of the storm from which the magic of Prospero is to rescue the souls on board.
3 Its technical terms are accurate. As the ship is driven before the wind the topsail is taken down and the topmast struck. As they near the shore the boatswain tries, with reefed foresail and mainsail, to gain sea-room, but the ship is blown bodily against the rocks. The presence of the Master of the ship is very slight; in the last scene of the play, when the rescued crew appear, he leaves all the talking to the boatswain, whose character dominates this brief episode.

**what cheer?** How are things with you?
**Good** Good fellow.
**yarely** Briskly.

**cheerly** Heartily.
**yare** Stand by.
**Tend to** Listen for.
**Blow till thou burst thy wind** Blow your utmost.
**if room enough** i.e. if only we have room to manoeuvre.
**have care** i.e. take care what you are doing.
**Play the men** More likely than 'have courage' is 'ply the men', urge them on.
**Do you not hear him?** Difficult to see in the storm, the master is to be heard blowing his whistle.
**assist the storm** i.e. by getting in the way.
**be patient** Because of the royal presence?
**counsellor** A member of the King's Council.
**work the peace of the presence** Restore the King's peace.
**hand** Handle.
**the mischance . . . so hap** The imminent disaster, should it so happen.
**his complexion is perfect gallows** i.e. he looks as if he is born to be hanged. Gonzalo is referring to the proverb, 'He who is born to be hanged will never be drowned.'
**Stand fast, good Fate** Gonzalo appeals to the goddess of destiny to be as good as her word (that the boatswain should be hanged).
**make the rope of his destiny our cable** i.e. make the means of his (future) execution our life-line.
**our own doth little advantage** i.e. our real cable (attached to the anchor) is of little use.
**main-course** Main-sail.
**office** i.e. shouted orders.
**give o'er** i.e. stop struggling to save the vessel.
**pox** A disease of the skin. Used here like the boatswain's 'A plague upon'.
**whoreson** An abusive word, literally meaning 'son of a whore'.
**unstanched** Suffering from a flow of blood.
**Lay her a-hold** Keep her close to the wind.
**two courses** i.e. main-sail and fore-sail.
**wide-chapp'd** i.e. having a face with broad 'chops' (the jaws as a prominent feature).
**The washing of ten tides!** i.e. like pirates hanged and then fastened to posts at low water in the Thames, till three tides had covered them. Antonio wishes the boatswain a slow death by actual drowning.
**gape at wid'st** More appropriate to an ocean wave than a mere drop of sea-water!
**glut** Swallow (archaic).
**The wills above** Divine will. Expressions like 'God's will' had been banned from the stage.

## Act I Scene 2

The transition from the raging storm and its shrieking victims to the secluded grotto (better in modern parlance than 'cell') is abrupt. Miranda's first words show she is aware of her magician father's powers and also that, despite her never having encountered other human beings in the past twelve years, she has a deep sense of compassion. In the methodical and even quizzical fashion he has probably followed in educating his daughter and sole heiress, Prospero first reassures her that all aboard are safe; then, knowing that his instructions for the rescue of the ship are being carried out by his spirit-servant Ariel, he doffs his magic robe and reveals to her for the first time the events which have led to their being stranded on a desert island. He has delayed telling the story until the arrival off the island (purely by chance as it has happened) of those responsible for his exile.

Returning across the Mediterranean Sea from Tunis, where his daughter has been married to the King – a fact not revealed until Act II and possibly not known to Prospero – Alonso of Naples, with all his companions in the chief vessel, has through his near approach to the island become subject to Prospero's magic. A specially created storm has separated the ship from the rest of the fleet and hurled it on the rocky coast. This is the hour Prospero chooses to inform Miranda who they really are.

Twelve years earlier her father was Duke of Milan, the leading dukedom of Italy, but so absorbed did he become in his studies, including magic, that he left all political control in the hands of his brother Antonio. In time Antonio conspired with the King of Naples to bring Milan into subjection to that monarch in return for help in seizing power and usurping the title from Prospero. After opening the gates one night to the Neapolitan troops, Antonio had Prospero and his infant daughter thrust into a leaky boat and launched upon the open sea. The villains dared not put his popular brother to death; on the other hand a loyal old courtier, Gonzalo, provided the deposed Duke with various necessaries, including his volume of magic. Prospero's abrupt and occasionally abrasive manner in this interview and the three which follow may be explained as caused by the tenseness of one whose spectacular operation, under astrological guidance, is aimed at a combination of triumph, revenge, reconciliation and political union.

Charming Miranda to sleep, he summons Ariel, the elemental

spirit whom he rescued from imprisonment and who now fulfils his miraculous orders. The description of the wrecking and the saving of the ship fills in the picture for the audience and prepares them for the appearance of some of the passengers and some of the crew.

Ariel murmuring at the next task awaiting him (the luring of Ferdinand to the scene) leads to Prospero's giving a detailed account of Caliban and his mother, the witch Sycorax, original owners of the otherwise uninhabited island. It is the turn of the misshapen savage to be summoned, uttering his complaints at his treatment: in return for information about the properties of the island, Prospero had at first given him some education, but then confined him to a rocky cave after he attempted to violate Miranda. Without any immediate cause being given for his appearance, apart from an exchange of incivilities, Caliban is dismissed to fetch in more fuel (presumably logs).

Lured on by Ariel's lyrics, Ferdinand approaches the grotto; Prospero bids Miranda open her eyes and watches with great pleasure the young couple's mutual admiration develop (his own magic operations now superfluous!). However, in order to render their spontaneous love steadfast, he decides to make their initial steps anything but smooth. Accusing Ferdinand of pretending to be a King (after his father's presumed death) and of acting as a spy, Prospero first immobilizes the prince's drawn sword and then marches him off to accommodation and food befitting a 'traitor', harshly ignoring the desperate entreaties of his daughter, who has just set eyes for the first time on an attractive young man. The infatuated Ferdinand proclaims that, if he can but behold through his cell window this lovely girl so different from the ladies of the court, he has no desire for other forms of liberty.

## *Commentary*

Of this exceptionally long scene the first half is devoted to a review of past events on the mainland; much of the second is taken up by the backgrounds of Ariel and Caliban. Prospero's story of his banishment is almost a monologue; three times he recalls Miranda from the abstraction into which the revelation of her birth has thrown her to what is, possibly to her island mind, an incomprehensible narrative of the internal politics of Milan.

These interruptions also help to rivet the attention of an audience whose thoughts might well be with the wreck.

The inaction of this part is then relieved by the entrance in turn of the magician's attendant spirit, swift to perform his commands in anticipation of release after years of service, and of his uncouth slave, grudging an obedience enforced by threat of cramps. The one is as sprightly and petulant as the other is clumsy and abusive. Both are given their tasks: Ariel, rather incongruously, is bidden to assume the guise of a sea-nymph and yet remain invisible to all but his master; Caliban must carry in still more fuel – a piling up of logs which seems strangely out of place in a warm climate.

From these two interviews the audience learns something of Prospero's magic powers since his arrival on the island, from the release of Ariel from the spell of Sycorax to the nightly torments of the unrepentant Caliban. Through the one he holds the spirit world at his beck and call, through the other he obtains the performance of those household tasks that are presumably too menial for a spirit's attention.

The scene reaches a climax of excitement in the first display of Prospero's own powers, as distinct from those of Ariel – the charming of Ferdinand, which anticipates that of his father in Act V.

One circumstance in this remarkable introductory scene is not clear from the text – Miranda's part in the haranguing of Caliban. At line 186 Prospero seems to impose sleep on her, by two lines of hypnotic suggestion, just as her interest is prompting further questions. It would seem that Miranda has never been aware of Ariel's existence, partly because the spirit is invisible to all save his master, partly because he has not been mentioned, so that this brief slumber may appear as unnecessary as Ariel's change of attire. However, while Miranda at other times might dismiss Prospero's words to empty air, it would be impossible to sustain this lengthy dialogue about the wreck and Sycorax in her conscious presence. Immediately after Ariel's departure Prospero wakens her to go on a visit with him to Caliban (a strange request); then he changes his mind and summons the slave to his presence. This is the moment chosen by Ariel for a brief reappearance in his nymph's disguise and we now understand that he is quite invisible to Miranda – unless indeed she has shut her eyes (1.312) to avoid beholding Caliban.

She could have remained thus until her father bids her

The fringed curtains of thine eye advance (l.411)

were it not that the Folio attributes to her the passage 'Abhorred slave . . . prison' (ll.353–364). Most editors have transferred these lines to Prospero, as more in keeping with his harsh pedagogic style. It would also be extraordinarily unnatural for what is a lengthy dissertation for such a young girl to come immediately after Caliban's coarse boast of the many children he might have begotten. Again it is difficult to imagine Miranda fulfilling a daily unremitting programme of linguistic training: far better to credit her with such simple gestures as pointing out the Man-in-the-Moon to this erstwhile companion (II,2,141). Caliban's hatred is reserved for her father; 'The red plague rid you' is obviously his retort to 'Deservedly confin'd into this rock'. Perhaps we should picture Miranda at 1.312 withdrawing to the far end of the grotto and closing her eyes or falling asleep until wakened at 1.411.

A minor obscurity is the 'other business' in ll.317 and 369, possibly forgotten in the dressing down of Caliban; or was the slave's encounter with Stephano and Trinculo and the ensuing 'foul conspiracy' actually another of Prospero's devices, like rousing a storm and then subduing it?

**Art** i.e. magic powers, associated with the mantle laid aside in 1.25.
**stinking pitch** From the blackness of the storm clouds.
**mounting to th' welkin's cheek** i.e. reaching as high as to pour over the 'cheek' (side-piece of a grate or furnace) and quench the fire which has been heating up the pitch. An extravagant poetic expression for a maiden isolated on an island – is it due to inheritance or tuition?
**brave** Fine.
**some noble creature** Unconscious anticipation.
**or ere** Before.
**fraughting souls** Human freight.
**Be collected** Calm yourself. Prospero's commands are all abrupt.
**amazement** Horror. A stronger word than now.
**piteous** Full of pity (for others).
**O, woe the day!** She does not at first comprehend her father's declaration (in itself quite 'amazing') that the vessel has not been harmed.
**more better** Double comparative, as often for emphasis in Elizabethan English.
**full** Very.
**meddle with my thoughts** i.e. occur to me.
**Lie there, my Art** Speaking to his mantle.

**direful spectacle** Dreadful sight.
**wrack** Wreck. Akin to 'rack and ruin'.
**virtue of compassion** Essence of pity.
**no soul —** Anacoluthon, or sentence broken off. 'Soul' has long been used of a life lost at sea instead of 'body', the least part of which is a single hair; here the 'perdition' (loss) of such a hair has intruded and taken over the main verb, substituting 'Betid' (happened) for 'was lost'.
**Which ... which** The antecedents are respectively 'creature' and 'vessel'.
**sink** In line 8 the vessel was 'dash'd all to pieces.'
**Sit down** Miranda has risen in her surprise. Another peremptory command.
**bootless inquisition** Vain questioning. Yet in line 21 she claimed she had never been curious to know.
**The very minute** More exact than the traditional 'hour' when destiny strikes and suited to a wreck which has been a matter of minutes.
**ope thine ear** His insistence on her close attention (instead of being distracted by the wreck) is repeated at intervals.
**Out three years** Fully three years.
**by any other house or person?** i.e. other than the grotto. Prospero wonders if she has any dim memory of Milan and its people, before he tells her anything about them.
**Of any thing ... remembrance** Describe any picture that you can recollect.
**an assurance ... warrants** A fact that my memory can vouch for.
**dark backward and abysm of time** Dimly recollected space of past years.
**How thou cam'st here** Such adult matters would dwell less in the very young memory than people immediately around her.
**Twelve year since** Twelve years ago. The old plural survives in dialect.
**piece of virtue** Masterpiece of chastity.
**thy father Was Duke of Milan** The double meaning (1) I, your father, was once the Duke, and (2) your father was, not I, but the Duke, illustrates Prospero's playful way of taking his hearer by surprise. The repetition (breaking off to answer her question) is intended to make clear that he is the former Duke, but it awkwardly breaks the connection of 'only heir and princess' with 'my daughter', to which it is in apposition.
**princess** Not a title, but like 'prince of power', a general term of rank.
**no worse issued** Born to the same high position (as her father).
**blessed** Miranda supposes that the peaceful island is a better place than the turbulent city; her father uses the word (1.63) in anticipation of her meeting with Ferdinand.
**heav'd** In using this more violent word is Prospero thinking of the brutal thrusting into a boat or simply the dangerous tossing of the waves, or both?
**holp hither** Helped on our way here. A reference to Gonzalo.

**teen** Woe, vexation.
**from my remembrance** Forgotten.
**to him put** Entrusted to him. The sentence is broken, like several others in this play. Prospero throughout the scene seems to be in a state of suppressed excitement.
**all the signories** All the lordships of Italy.
**prime duke** Milan was the leading dukedom.
**liberal Arts** Intellectual studies.
**to my state grew stranger** Lost all connection with the government of my dukedom.
**secret studies** Contemporary magic.
**perfected how to grant suits** Experienced in granting applications.
**trash** Hold back (with a leash). A hunting term, this is the opposite of 'advance' (urge forward), as 'deny' is the opposite of 'grant'.
**over-topping** i.e. being too ambitious.
**new created** Reappointed (in his own interests).
**chang'd 'em** i.e. appointed others in their places.
**new form'd 'em** Converted them to his own opinions.
**key** The metaphor changes from the key which opens an office (with access to the office-holder) to the key which then tuned an instrument.
**suck'd my verdure out on't** i.e. like a parasite fed on the sap in my trunk which kept my foliage green. A further change of metaphor.
**thus neglecting worldly ends ... rate** Prospero's habit of repeating himself (cf. ll. 74–7) leads here to obscure phrasing. The meaning of this long participial phrase seems to be: 'by ceasing to carry out my ducal functions in order to concentrate on studies which, except that they withdrew me from the public gaze, were more valuable than anything more popular with the crowd.' The subject of 'Awak'd' is 'I' in 1.89.
**Like a good parent** This simile (from what may happen in the best regulated families) gives plainer expression to the personification of his trust begetting a son as false as his father was true. Prospero's limitless confidence was to be equalled by unlimited treachery.
**in its contrary** Directly opposite in character.
**sans bound** Without limits. This obsolete borrowing from the French is familiar in the last line of the well-known Seven Ages Speech in *As You Like It*: 'Sans teeth, sans eyes, sans taste, sans everything'.
**lorded** Created (de facto) lord.
**what my power might else exact** What other advantage was to be gained by the exercise of my authority.
**like one ... lie** Not a simile, but a comparison, probably made more difficult by faulty type. The intended meaning could be: 'like one who, by constantly repeating a lie has come to regard it (to himself) as the truth and made his memory into a false liar.'
**he did believe** Is Prospero making a psychological excuse for his brother's villainy?
**out o' th' substitution** Arising from the replacement of Prospero. The

**main verb** of this broken sentence is 'needs' in line 108.
**executing... of royalty** i.e. performing the ducal ceremonies, while not being the Duke.
**no screen** i.e. no further nominal distinction between duke in name and duke in fact.
**Absolute Milan** i.e. the reigning duke.
**temporal royalties** Ducal functions.
**confederates** Conspires.
**So dry he was for sway** He was so thirsty for power.
**poor Milan** Referring this time to the state and not its ruler.
**O the heavens!** Her favourite maidenly exclamation (also 'alack').
**Mark his condition... event** Take note of this political agreement and what resulted from it (Prospero is coming to this).
**If this might be a brother** Whether a (true) brother could have done such a thing.
**in lieu o' th' premises** In return for the terms laid down in the 'condition' (i.e. homage and tribute to Naples).
**Of homage... tribute** Note the repetition (of 1.113) so characteristic of Prospero.
**presently** Immediately.
**A treacherous army levied** By Alonso.
**a hint... eyes to 't** A cause sad enough to bring the tears to my eyes at the thought of it.
**present business** i.e. the wreck, which has been distracting her attention.
**impertinent** irrelevant. A strange conception that only the magically induced wreck can give their past history relevance!
**wench** Once a polite term. Even so, Prospero is talking like a strict pedagogue.
**With colours... foul ends** Disguised their wicked intention: to put us to death by means short of actual murder.
**hurried us aboard a bark** Shakespeare seems unaware that Milan is not a sea-port.
**butt** Cask. Used contemptuously for a small boat.
**loving wrong** A strange example of oxymoron, or even pathetic fallacy: the winds (often personified in classical poetry) blew with more affection than force.
**deck'd** (1) covered, (2) ornamented. This far-fetched metaphor includes the idea of adding salt water to salt water!
**Under my burthen groan'd** i.e. (have) groaned at my heavy fate.
**undergoing stomach** Enduring courage.
**By providence divine** By God's provision (which is divine – tautology). By the time of this play the name of God was forbidden in stage use.
**charity** Loving care (the original meaning).
**Rich garments** Later used to tempt certain evil-doers.
**steaded much** Been of good service.
**gentleness** Well-bred courtesy.

**Act I Scene 2 29**

**ever** i.e. at some time.
**Now I arise** Prospero dons his mantle to summon Ariel, invisible to all but his master, and, of course, the audience. The 'last of our sea-sorrow' is very briefly told.
**can** i.e. can derive more profit (from their tutoring).
**vainer hours** i.e. hours in which to indulge in less serious matters.
**not so careful** Less conscientious.
**By accident... this shore** The accident is not the storm but the course on which the ship was navigated; this piece of good fortune brought them within the limited sphere of his magic powers.
**prescience** Foreknowledge.
**A most auspicious star** Predictions based on omens began with 'auspicium', lit. 'bird-watching', and later followed the movements of stars (astrology).
**If now I court not** If I do not pay instant attention to.
**a good dulness** A welcome torpor. It would provide rest after a lengthy discourse and leave him free to deliver another to an invisible auditor.
**And give it way** And so give in to it.
**All hail... hail!** Chiasmus (see *Literary Terms*).
**To answer thy best pleasure** To satisfy your most exacting desire. If 'to fly' belongs to the sphere of earth, Ariel is boasting of his prowess in all four elements: earth, water, fire and air.
**quality** i.e. fellow-spirits.
**to point** Down to the last detail.
**every article** i.e. every item mentioned in your commands.
**beak** Bow.
**the waist** Amidships.
**flam'd amazement** Made lightning strike horror into the beholders. St Elmo's fire played about the tops of ships' masts during a storm.
**distinctly** i.e. as separate flames.
**Jove's lightnings** The prerogative of Jupiter, Roman king of the gods.
**precursors** Forerunners.
**sight-outrunning** i.e. disappearing almost before being glimpsed.
**cracks** Loud explosive noises, here thunder-claps.
**sulphurous** The sulphur is taken from the 'crack' of cannon, not from celestial thunder.
**most mighty Neptune** Ironic reference to the Roman god of the sea.
**dread trident** Neptune was regularly pictured with this three-pronged spear.
**coil** Tumult.
**infect his reason** Drive him mad.
**play'd... of desperation** Did strange things in their despair.
**All but mariners** All except the crew (who would in any case know better). This separation was devised by Prospero.
**sustaining** i.e. which had supported them in the water. An erroneous belief.
**blemish** Stain (from salt water). For the miraculous 'freshness' cf.II, 1, 60.

**by himself** A specific 'article' in Prospero's instructions.
**odd angle** Out-of-the-way corner.
**in this sad knot** Ariel mimics the dejected prince.
**Of the King's ... mariners** One more inversion: 'The mariners of the King's ship.' One disposition was not contrived by the magician, the encounter of Caliban with two members of this crew, or could this be the 'other business' hinted at later on (1.317)?
**deep nook** Deep-water creek.
**still-vex'd Bermoothes** The Bermudas, plagued by storms. A long distance for a small matter of dew (these islands have a moist climate), required in a magical experiment (See *Sources*, p.15).
**a charm join'd ... labour** A spell superimposed on physical exhaustion.
**flote** Sea.
**What is the time o' th' day?** With an hour-glass the only means of reckoning the passage of time on the island, this question seems pointless, except to let the audience know.
**'twixt six and now** We should say 'between now and six.'
**preciously** Valuably.
**Is there more toil?** This grudging remark contrasts with his breezy readiness to perform any and every task in 1.190!
**remember thee** Remind you. Ariel uses the familiar second singular to his master – a 'tricksy spirit' indeed. Perhaps his cheeky attitude is a device to introduce a full account of his origin and that of Caliban.
**moody?** Why are you in such a mood? Or is this an epithet for a creature of as many moods as there are elements?
**bate me** Reduce my service by.
**think'st it much** i.e. find it too hard work.
**tread the ooze ... sharp wind ... bak'd with frost** Three elements, but in their harsher aspects, regarded by Prospero as a relief from painful imprisonment.
**envy** Malice.
**Where was she born?** Prospero's schoolmasterly interrogation continues to convey information to the audience.
**Argier** Algiers. In Shakespeare's day it had a bad enough reputation as a centre of piracy.
**Once in a month** Not a regular curriculum, but a general phrase indicating the short memory of a sprite, though Ariel's experiences seem sufficiently unforgettable!
**For mischiefs manifold ... terrible** This line, packed with polysyllables, and its two epithets following their respective substantives, has a sinister ring.
**one thing she did** This remains a mystery.
**blue-ey'd** With blue rings round the eyes – a sign of pregnancy.
**As thou report'st thyself** According to your own account.
**hests** Commands.
**potent ministers** Powerful agents.

**unmitigable** Whose severity nothing could soften.
**rift** Narrow cleft.
**as fast as mill-wheels strike** Water-mills (much older than windmills) were driven by the force of the mill-stream against the paddles, which would strike the water as the wheel revolved.
**whelp** The young of certain wild animals, especially the lion. Then used contemptuously of a bad-mannered youth.
**not honour'd ... shape** This refers not to Caliban, but to the island, lacking inhabitants.
**Dull thing** Prospero resents being anticipated; 'dull' is even more unfair than 'malignant' (1.257).
**in service** As a domestic servant (slave 1.310).
**wolves ... bears** Without any indication of the size of the island or any mention of natural features, except some typically English gorse-bushes and stagnant pools, we must accept these hints of prowling beasts as credulously as we do the stately goddesses in the masque in Act IV.
**damn'd** Those condemned to hell for their sins.
**an oak** By its knotty nature making a worse punishment than being imprisoned in a pine; twelve winters would add to the severity.
**correspondent** Obedient.
**spriting** Work as an elemental spirit.
**gently** In well-behaved fashion.
**like a nymph o' the sea** A pointless piece of masquing, to indulge Prospero's passion for such performances displayed in Act IV.
**hence With diligence** i.e. be off and pay every attention to what I have commanded.
**Heaviness** More easily explained as the effect of her father's art (1.186).
**miss** Do without.
**Fine apparition** Congratulating Ariel on his disguise. Is there a dramatic intention to highlight Caliban's deformity by contrast?
**quaint** Dainty.
**Hark in thine ear** Instructions about Ferdinand, whose arrival is to come as a surprise.
**dew** The magic substance sought for (1.228).
**raven** A bird of ill omen.
**south-west** The south-west wind was associated with sickness.
**Side-stitches** Pains between the ribs making breathing difficult.
**urchins** Hedgehogs. Nocturnal creatures credited with mischievous pranks.
**for that vast of night that they may work** i.e. in the long hours of darkness during which they are allowed to be active (from curfew till cock-crow). Duration is a feature of Prospero's punishments.
**all exercise** i.e. all of them practise their torments.
**As thick as honeycomb** Another reference to nature: the closeness of the cells suggests the comparison of the pinches to bee-stings.

**'em** The cells of the honeycomb.
**Thou strok'st me** Caliban uses the familiar second singular when reflecting on his past as a pupil, but the second plural in his present condition as a slave.
**Water with berries in 't** Possibly coffee.
**qualities** Good points.
**sty me** Shut me in (now used only of pigs).
**human** Humane.
**Abhorred slave** Lines 353–64 in the Folio are spoken by Miranda; they are best transferred to Prospero (see *Commentary* to this scene).
**print** Impression.
**race** Nature.
**learn** i.e. acquire some book knowledge.
**my profit on 't** The advantage I have gained from it.
**The red plague** Bubonic plague (accompanied by red or purple spots). There was an outbreak in London in 1606.
**learning** Teaching (originally this word had both senses, cf. 1.361).
**rack** Lit. torture by stretching the joints.
**old cramps** (1) such as afflict old people, (2) a lot of them.
**Setebos** According to 16th-century travellers, the chief god of the Patagonians in South America.
*whist* Being hushed. A reference to peace after the storm, as the next lyric deals with a consequence of it?
*featly* Gracefully.
**Burthen** Refrain.
**passion** Grief.
**That the earth owes** Belonging to this world.
**The fringed curtains ... advance** Open your eyes. This suggests that Miranda *has* been kept in a trance at least since the entry of Caliban.
**beauty's canker** The disease, or the grub, that destroys the beauty of a flower.
**airs** Tunes.
**remain** Dwell.
**my prime request ... pronounce** i.e. my third and last question is the most important. It is curious that Ferdinand's opening remarks are made in the elaborate diction of the court before he finds out whether they speak the same language! Even more curiously coincidental is his addressing her as a 'wonder' when the name Miranda means 'one who arouses admiration'.
**the King of Naples** Whom Ferdinand believes drowned, but Prospero knows to be alive.
**A single thing** i.e. a solitary survivor.
**He does hear me** i.e. I hear *myself* (and weep for it).
**never since at ebb** i.e. flowing with tears ever since. A good maritime metaphor.
**fit** The right time.
**chang'd eyes** Fallen in love.

**you have done yourself some wrong**  You have put yourself at risk by your action.
**affection not gone forth**  Love not bestowed.
**both in either's pow'rs**  i.e. a mutual control, founded on feeling, not magic.
**swift business**  i.e. headlong falling in love.
**uneasy**  Difficult (the original meaning).
**attend**  (1) follow me, (2) listen to what I have to say.
**thou ow'st not**  You do not possess.
**temple**  Frequent metaphor for the body as the dwelling-place of the spirit.
**strive to dwell with 't**  Unlike with the unprepossessing Caliban!
**fresh-brook mussels**  Freshwater mussels are unfit to eat.
**entertainment**  Treatment.
**gentle, and not fearful**  Another ambiguity: either (1) well-bred and therefore nothing to be afraid of (or not timid), or (2) mild in character and therefore nobody to fear. Miranda is too aware of her father's magic powers to be anxious on his account.
**My foot my tutor?**  i.e. am I to take advice from one so ignorant (of men's affairs)? Harsh words indeed to the daughter he is steering into a love-match! More is to come.
**come from thy ward**  Lower your sword.
**this stick**  The magician's wand (which later he breaks in token of abandoning his powers).
**An advocate . . . impostor!**  Do you intend to plead for one who falsely pretends to be a king?
**hush!**  i.e. stop complaining!
**To th' most of men**  Compared with the majority.
**nerves**  Sinews.
**bound up**  Held fast in prison (see 1.493).
**through my prison**  i.e. from my prison window.
**unwonted**  Most unusual.

## Revision questions on Act I

**1** What does the first scene reveal of the characters who figure in the play?
**2** Tell with as much detail as you can the story of Prospero prior to his arrival on the island.
**3** Would it be better if Scene 2 were divided into two or more scenes?
**4** To how many people is Prospero abrupt? Give reasons for his manner.

## Act II Scene 1

Miraculously preserved from the wreck and unharmed by the sea, the Neapolitan court make nevertheless a dejected group on shore, with the king's son missing, believed drowned. The King is inconsolable, in spite of the efforts of old Gonzalo to make him appreciate his deliverance and admire the pleasant aspect of the island. He is supported by Adrian and Francisco and mocked, apart, by Sebastian the King's brother, and Antonio, Prospero's usurping brother. When Alonso refuses to be encouraged by Francisco's account of Ferdinand swimming ashore, this precious pair blame the disaster on Alonso's previous determination to marry his daughter across the sea to an African king. Then, as if to distract attention from a painful topic, Gonzalo launches out on an idealistic but largely negative picture of the primitive society he would establish, were he king of the island (whose constitution would not include a sovereign!).

Gonzalo's Golden Age having been dismissed by the King as an irrelevance, the old man declares he has merely been providing his mockers with something to laugh at. At this point Ariel enters and all except Antonio and Sebastian are put into a trance, the last to go under being Alonso, who is persuaded by the two villains to accept the drowsiness as relief from sorrow, while they keep guard.

Using the dreamlike atmosphere as a cover for proposing such a cold-blooded scheme, Antonio gradually persuades Sebastian to seize this golden opportunity and join him in killing Alonso and Gonzalo, so securing the kingdom of Naples for Sebastian and independence for his own duchy of Milan. Sebastian seems to need a lot of explanation for one who has just been lavishing witticisms on Gonzalo; however, when he recollects something similar having happened in Milan, he readily consents. Ariel reappears in the nick of time and sings a song of warning in Gonzalo's ear, so that he wakes and rouses the King, who is astonished to see the two would-be murderers standing white-faced and with drawn swords. Sebastian quickly explains his posture as caused by the loud roaring of some wild animals.

Apparently convinced, the despairing Alonso leads them off in renewed search for his son, Gonzalo being as confident the young man has escaped drowning as he was over the boatswain's destiny.

## Commentary

The conventional Elizabethan word-play in the first part of this scene, with its impromptu and brisk retorts, tedious to modern ears, is in effective contrast with the series of solemn and factual speeches we have just listened to. We are now given two pictures: one of the Prince (imprisoned not drowned) breasting the waves, the other Gonzalo's blue-print for his 'commonwealth'. The latter is remarkable for the complete absence of all features of urban civilization, particularly crime and organized warfare – exactly, in fact, the state of the island without, however, the imagined population living in pristine innocence and habitual idleness on the ample products of unaided Nature. Such speculation was typical of Shakespeare's day, as a result of the impact of European civilization on primitive races (Scene 2 is not without some bearing on the problem created by the sale of liquor to natives). Ironically, Gonzalo presupposes that treason and the drawing of swords would be unknown, yet in the space of a brief quarter of an hour he is to come face to face with both.

The lengthy prompting of Sebastian by Antonio with its subtle suggestions, cautious hints and discreet comparisons, leads up to an exciting climax. However, by now the audience is aware that events are all pre-ordained 'to every article' by Prospero, whether the tempting and preventing of the guilty brothers or the parallel frustration of Caliban and his fellow-conspirators.

**merry** Cheerful (without modern hilarity).
**beyond our loss** Gonzalo values personal salvation above bereavement.
**hint** Cause.
**some merchant** Some trading vessel.
**visitor** An allusion to the parish visitor who calls on the needy.
**tell** Count (the strokes). Early watches were in use in the 16th century.
**When every grief ... entertainer** i.e. if one harbours every sorrow that life brings, one will be constantly subjected to ... Here Sebastian punningly interjects 'A dollar', meaning payment for the 'entertainer', whereupon Gonzalo, not to be outdone, finds another pun to complete his sentence, 'dolour' being a synonym for 'pain'.
**dollar** An old European coin which migrated to North America.
**A laughter** When Antonio wonders who will speak first, the 'old cock' (Gonzalo) or 'the cockerel' (Adrian), they place a wager, won by Antonio, who is paid by laughing at Sebastian's expense. The Folio gives 'So you're paid' to Antonio, which must be erroneous.
**Temperance** To Adrian 'temperature', to Antonio a girl's name, a Puritanical one, like Prudence and Grace.

## 36 The Tempest

**subtle** Cunning.
**an eye** A speck.
**misses not much** i.e. detects the small 'eye'.
**mistake the truth totally** i.e. gets the rest of it wrong. A stupid pun.
**As many vouch'd rarities are** i.e. the genuinely rare is usually 'incredible'.
**glosses** Shining surfaces.
**pocket up** A derived meaning: 'pigeon-holing the result of an investigation.'
**prosper well** Ironical.
**a paragon to** A perfect model as.
**widow Dido** Popularly thought of as simply the lover of Aeneas, she was a princess of Tyre who, after the murder of her husband, sailed across the Mediterranean to found Carthage in North Africa, future rival of Rome. Rather than be forced to marry a local king, she sacrificed herself on a funeral pyre.
**'widower Aeneas'** As told in Virgil's *Aeneid*, this Trojan prince, after the famous sack of the city, eventually settled in Italy as the founder of the Roman race. In Carthage he and Dido fell in love but he deserted her in pursuit of his destiny, and she immolated herself. Though 300 years actually separated them, this became one of the world's great love-stories. There was no marriage, fictional or otherwise.
**study of that** Consider it again.
**Carthage** The ruined site of the Carthaginian capital is about ten miles from the later city of Tunis.
**miraculous harp** An ancient legend of city walls being built by supernatural music, e.g. Amphion's harp raised those of Thebes and Apollo's those of Troy.
**Ay** A delayed affirmative of his identification of Carthage with Tunis before turning to speak to Alonso; or perhaps a sign of contempt for the running commentary of Antonio and Sebastian.
**Bate** Leaving out.
**That sort was well fish'd for** That qualification took some time to come out, like landing a difficult fish.
**against ... of my sense** Making my sense of hearing revolt.
**surges** Swelling waves.
**contentious** i.e. contesting his progress.
**wave-worn basis** The foot of the cliffs eroded by the waves.
**loose** Lose. Claribel's uncle is protesting against a diplomatic marriage to a black ruler forced upon his niece.
**at least** i.e. at the least harmful, compared with your present loss.
**who hath ... grief on't** (You) who have, in the loss of Ferdinand, good reason to shed tears over the separation from Claribel.
**Weigh'd ... bow** The meaning is clear, but the expression faulty. Claribel's fate depended like a balance on which pan, reluctance to marry or obedience to her father, should weigh the heavier and so

sink that end of the beam. 'She' is understood in 'should bow', i.e. bend in submission (unlike the movement of a balance).
**dear'st** Most precious part.
**The truth you speak . . . in** You have adopted a harsh manner and chosen the wrong time to speak the truth.
**Very well** Have it your own way.
**chirurgeonly** Spoken like a good surgeon.
**plantation** Gonzolo is using the word in terms of 'colonizing' but Sebastian and Antonio understand it in its literal sense.
**I' th' commonwealth** Nowhere does a passage of Shakespeare appear closer to its source than this to the following lines, quoted here for comparison. They were taken from Florio's translation of Montaigne's *Essais* (1603), Vol.1, chap.31, 'Of the Cannibals' (Spanish corruption of the Caribs of the Caribbean Islands).

It is a nation . . . that hath no kinde of traffike, no knowledge of letters, no intelligence of numbers, no name of magistrate, nor of politike superioritie, no use of service, of riches, or of poverty; no contracts, no successions, no partitions, no occupation but idle; no respect of kindred, but common, no apparell but naturall, no manuring of lands, no use of wine, corne or mettle. The very words that import lying, falshood, treason, dissimulation, covetousness, envie, detraction, and pardon were never heard of amongst them.

**by contraries** In ways exactly the opposite of what is usually found.
**Letters** Learning.
**succession** i.e. to property.
**Bourn** Boundary; 'bound' is practically a synonym.
**engine** i.e. of war.
**foison** Abundance. Further tautology.
**nothing** Empty nonsense.
**minister occasion** Provide an opportunity.
**sensible** Sensitive.
**use** Are accustomed.
**flat-long** i.e. striking with the flat of the sword, therefore harmless.
**sphere** In the Ptolemaic system the sun, moon and planets revolved each in a separate crystal sphere around the earth.
**bat-fowling** Bird-hunting on moonless nights, with a light to dazzle them and a 'bat' (club) to knock them down with.
**good my lord** Addressed to Gonzalo.
**adventure my discretion so weakly** Risk my reputation for discretion by being so foolish (as to get angry).
**hear us** i.e. in your sleep.
**Would, with themselves . . . thoughts** i.e. stop me thinking as well as seeing.
**I find** His wish is granted.
**th' occasion speaks thee** The opportunity cries out to you. This speech contains the broadest of hints, yet it takes all of Antonio's eloquence to

## 38 The Tempest

bring the point home. Sebastian is not stupid, nor is *he* weighing himself in the balance between loyalty and treachery: the prolonged discussion simply keeps the audience in suspense.

**a sleepy language** i.e. the words of a dreamer who has strange visions.

**wink'st . . . art waking** i.e. you shut your eyes to opportunities while physically awake.

**if heed me** 'You' is understood.

**which to do** What I would advise.

**standing water** i.e. at the turn of the tide.

**to ebb . . . instructs me** i.e. I am by nature too lazy to 'flow' (act in my own interests).

**If you but knew . . . invest it!** You should realize that you are fostering in your mind the very idea you are ridiculing; by divesting it of any seriousness you are actually investing it with importance. (In other words your flippancy is a mask to your set intention – the argument is floundering in deep water).

**Ebbing men . . . sloth** Those on the way down (i.e. without spirit or enterprise) risk complete failure through sheer timidity or laziness.

**setting** Fixed expression.

**throes thee much to yield** i.e. costs you pain (or mental effort) to produce.

**Thus** Here it is.

**of as little memory** As little remembered (after death) as he is now capable of remembering.

**a spirit of persuasion . . . persuade** Persuasion itself, but without any belief in what he is stating.

**no hope that way . . . there** No hope for his survival is a hope for something so high that ambition cannot see beyond it, or expect to find anything there if it could.

**Ten leagues beyond man's life** Hyperbole. The distance from Tunis to Naples is about 350 miles (560 km).

**note** Letter.

**were post** Carried the letter. The early system of communication was by relays of horses at posts along the road.

**till new-born chins . . . razorable** Till infants are young men. The reason for this exaggeration is not clear; Antonio is magnifying the distance out of all proportion.

**from whom** Leaving whom.

**cast** Cast up by the sea but, by a pun, taken as actors 'cast' for parts in a play to which the storm has been the prologue.

**what to come** Future developments (are).

**What stuff is this!** Is Sebastian being 'slothful' in the face of action, or slow in the uptake, or intent on extracting the maximum of reasons from Antonio to assuage his 'conscience'? (cf. 1.270).

**some space** Admittedly a certain distance.

**cubit** An ancient measure of varying length, from 16 to 24 inches (40–60 cms).

**Measure us** Travel the whole distance measured by us, the cubits.
**them** i.e. the sleepers.
**chough** Jackdaw.
**And how ... good fortune?** And what value does your happiness put on this stroke of luck?
**feater** More elegant. Double comparative.
**But for** With the exception of.
**kibe** Chilblain.
**deity** i.e. worshipped by others.
**candied be they ... molest** May they be sweetened and softened (to weaken any resistance) before they trouble me.
**the perpetual wink for aye** Death.
**Should not upbraid our course** i.e. would not disapprove of our action if he were dead (which he would do if alive).
**tell the clock to** i.e. co-operate with.
**that ... the hour** That we find expedient.
**I the King** i.e. King-to-be.
**his project dies** i.e. his plan (for the exposure of Alonso and the final reconciliation) will fail.
*Open-ey'd* i.e. not induced to sleep (like the intended victims).
**awake?** The King is surprised to find they have not been sleeping too. As they had offered to stay awake on guard, lines 303–304 seem more appropriate, as emended in some editions, to Gonzalo.
**That's verily** That's true.

## Act II Scene 2

Bearing his slave's burden of firewood, Caliban loudly curses his master, though aware that Prospero's servant spirits may hear him: he is caught in a vicious circle – his torments make him utter curses, but their utterance only leads to further torments. He declares that these native spirits play their tricks on him, their fellow-islander, only at the bidding of the magician who punishes him, so he alleges, for the slightest offence.

When Trinculo, stranded court jester, appears, Caliban takes him for another spirit and lies flat on the ground in his fear. Trinculo, concerned by signs of another storm, comes across the strange creature huddled under his loose gaberdine; he has just come to the conclusion that it is an islander struck down in the storm when a thunder-clap drives him to seek shelter in the only place available – under the native's cloak.

The ship's butler (i.e. bottler) Stephano arrives, the worse for drink (from a keg on which he has floated ashore). Asserting he is not to be daunted by four-legged monsters, he responds to Caliban's cry for mercy by plying him with drink. Trinculo recognizes the voice of a friend he has thought drowned and fears that the two voices are those of devils. When Stephano in turn recognizes Trinculo's voice, he pulls the jester from beneath the cloak.

Having related their escapes to each other they listen to Caliban's expressions of worship of a deity descended from the moon upon his island. He also offers to show them where to find food (of bare subsistence standard) in their wild surroundings. Stephano, assuming that he and Trinculo are the sole survivors from the wreck, pronounces his accession to the sovereignty of the island, with one sworn 'subject' now addicted to the bottle, and another scornful of a 'monster' rendering abject homage to a drunkard. The procession of three sets off unsteadily for yet 'another part of the island'.

## Commentary

A complete contrast in behaviour to that of the previous scene, and welcome comic relief after an atmosphere of cynical wit and treacherous scheming. More, too, of Shakespeare's parallels:

1 Kings of the island: the sovereignty suffers a 'sea-change' from the constitutional creation of Gonzalo to a butler sitting on a keg of wine.

2 Two conspiracies: parallel with the attempt to assassinate the real king is the stirring of revolt against the real ruler of the island.

3 Two mistaken beliefs: Alonso thinks Ferdinand is drowned, Stephano thinks the same of Trinculo.

As a comic sub-plot this scene is differentiated from Scene 1 in employing prose instead of verse – the 'upstairs and downstairs' of Elizabethan stage dialogue. It is interesting to note how Caliban's opening soliloquy in blank verse (followed immediately by the jester's communings in prose) turns to snatches of both prose and verse in his exchanges with the other two, and reverts to blank verse to announce the transfer of his allegiance; he even achieves an impromptu lyric, as if in rivalry of Ariel.

This lyric mentions two ways in which the natives were of service to planters: catching the local fish and piling up supplies of wood. The scene's dominant factor is one which only later generations have been able to appreciate – the impact of alcohol on primitive races.

**flats** Swamps (archaic).
**By inch-meal** Inch by inch. Cf. piecemeal.
**urchin shows** Goblin apparitions.
**like a firebrand** i.e. in the form of a will-o'-the-wisp.
**every trifle** i.e. every trivial offence.
**mow** Makes faces. Cf. the old doublet, 'mop and mow'.
**mount...footfall** Erect their spines when they hear me coming.
**wound with** Surrounded by.
**bear off** Shelter me from.
**bombard** Large black leathern flagon, in shape like a 'bombard' or primitive cannon.
**Poor-John** Hake dried and salted.
**painted** i.e. representation on a sign outside of the monster within.
**make a man** Make my fortune.
**doit** A small coin of little worth.
**dead Indian** i.e. a native of the West Indies, brought by explorers to England for exhibition and frequently succumbing to the climate.
**gaberdine** Cloak of coarse material.
**shroud** Take shelter.
**at a man's funeral** Presuming his friend Trinculo has been drowned.
**swabber** Man in charge of swabbing the decks.
**put tricks upon's** i.e. astound us with strange sights.
**salvages** Natives.
**on four legs** Stephano adapts the hackneyed phrase 'on two legs' to the spectacle before him.
**an ague** Both 'salvages' are shaking with anxiety.
**some relief** i.e. help from his bottle.
**neat's leather** Cow-hide, i.e. leather shoes.
**too much for him** i.e. an excessive fortune.
**he shall pay...soundly** He (to whom I sell the 'monster') shall pay me a goodly sum.
**trembling** He mistakes Stephano's unsteadiness for possession by an evil spirit.
**cat** Alluding to the proverb, 'Good liquor will make a cat speak.'
**shake your shaking** Stop your trembling.
**chaps** Chops. See note on I,1,56.
**Amen!** i.e. finish drinking!
**siege** Sitting-end.
**moon-calf** A false conception, believed to be caused by the moon; hence any congenital idiot.
**vent** Discharge (from his body).
**constant** Settled.
**butt of sack** Barrel of wine.

**the bark of a tree** By the skill of a 'bottler'.
**Here** Giving Caliban a drink.
**kiss the book** i.e. have a drink from the bottle, perhaps suggested by 'swearing on the bottle'.
**when time was** In days gone by.
**My mistress** Miranda's teaching was more homely than her father's learned distinction between the sun and the moon. The legendary human figure discerned on the face of the moon, with dog and thorn-bush, plays a part in the comic interlude of 'Pyramus and Thisbe' in *A Midsummer Night's Dream*, Act V.
**new contents** i.e. fresh wine. Pun on the 'contents' of a book.
**this is a very shallow monster** The beginning of Trinculo's hostility towards Caliban.
**Well drawn** That was a good draught.
**puppy-headed** Empty-headed.
**crabs** Crab-apples.
**pig-nuts** The bulb-like roots of a wild plant, which have a nutty taste, but are not easily dug up.
**marmoset** A kind of monkey named after some grotesque figures in marble.
**scamels** Possibly a misprint for 'sea-mells', i.e. sea-mews or gulls.
**inherit** Take possession.
*No more dams* The secret of dam-making in the American colonies was known only to Indians.
*scrape trenchering* Scrub dishes.
**high-day** The same as 'hey-day', an expression of exultation.

## Revision questions on Act II

**1** Describe in as much detail as you can Gonzalo's ideal commonwealth.

**2** Explain how Alonso's court came to be wrecked on the island.

**3** Show by stages how Antonio persuades Sebastian to join him in killing Alonso and Gonzalo.

**4** Portray Stephano and Trinculo as seen by Caliban.

## Act III Scene 1

Ferdinand is describing to himself how the menial task of log-piling has been turned into a labour of love by Miranda with her half-hourly stolen visits. She believes her father to be engaged in his studies, though he has actually appeared backstage to observe the progress of his love-plot. Declining her offer to do some carrying for him, Ferdinand asks her name, rather belatedly. He thinks 'Miranda' (in Italian 'wonderful one') most appropriate for one who exceeds in her perfection all other women he has met. Admitting her own relative ignorance of men, she declares she would prefer him as a companion above all others. Having been drawn to her at first sight he is content to forget his rank and perform his slavish duties for her sake.

Her simple question 'Do you love me?' contrasts with the courtly phrasing of his response. Weeping modestly at her 'unworthiness', she makes the offer of marriage before he does, a further contrast with the social conventions of faraway Naples. They hold hands in agreement and part for another brief space of time, leaving Prospero to rejoice before returning to his other schemes.

## *Commentary*

Prospero's role as magician has entailed much looking-on as events unfold, with frequent comments, now of approval, now of a caustic satisfaction. Few other characters in Shakespeare employ so many asides.

This love-making scene is one of tender beauty and simplicity: the sophisticated courtier prince and the desert-island-reared maiden meet on common ground, subject to no other magic than personal attraction. Youthful sincerity is a radiant counter-balance to hypocrisy and artifice, savage instincts and drunken buffoonery. It does not do to point out that he tells her twice that he is Prince of Naples, while delaying till the second visit before asking her name!

**There be some sports . . . sets off** Some amusements involve hard toil, but the enjoyment they bring offsets this. The reader of this play needs to be on the alert for such inverted sentences (e.g. object before subject).
**nobly undergone** Stoically endured.
**most poor matters . . . rich ends** i.e. the humblest tasks can lead to fortunes.
**quickens** Makes alive.
**Upon a sore injunction** With the warning of severe punishment for disobedience.
**I forget** i.e. to do my work (lost in his thoughts).
**Most busilest when I do it** i.e. such thoughts are most active in my mind when I am engaged on this work. He has started on the logs

**44 The Tempest**

again with renewed effort; when Miranda appears she protests at such exertion. This 'prize textual crux', as it has been called, is thoroughly dealt with in the New Arden Edition pp. 71–3. Shakespeare may have given 'busily' a special superlative and a typical double one at that – a real mouthful for emphasis!

**when this burns** When this log you are carrying is in the fire (which will cause the gum to run).
**He's safe for these three hours** Dramatic irony.
**Poor worm** Poor creature.
**broke your hest to say so** Disobeyed your command (1) not to give it, (2) by giving it.
**several virtues** i.e. each had her particular good point.
**ow'd** Possessed.
**put it to the foil** Caused its defeat.
**skilless** Ignorant.
**to like of** To be attracted to.
**condition** Rank.
**flesh-fly** Blow-fly.
**this sound** i.e. the word 'love'.
**crown what I profess . . . event** i.e. bless my professed love with a happy outcome (marriage?)
**hollowly** Falsely.
**invert . . . mischief!** i.e. change my fortune from good to evil.
**What I desire to give** i.e. my love.
**What I shall die to want** i.e. your love.
**it** i.e. my passion.
**I'll die your maid** i.e. marrying no other. Notice the parallel antitheses: wife and maid, fellow and servant.
**your fellow** Your (social) equal.
**My mistress** i.e. *not* my servant.
**as willing as bondage . . . freedom** As willing as a slave to have his freedom.
**A thousand thousand!** 'Farewells' understood.
**surpris'd** i.e. taken by surprise (love at first sight), whereas the delight of Prospero, who has planned it, is less intense.
**my rejoicing . . . more** Nothing gives me greater cause for rejoicing.
**appertaining** Related to the young couple (the masque in Act IV) or perhaps the 'banquet' in Scene 3.

## Act III Scene 2

For some reason Stephano keeps his newly recruited subject well supplied with drink from a limited store. Trinculo mocks and insults the wretched Caliban, who is invited by 'King' Stephano to present his 'suit'. This is a plan to catch Prospero asleep, kill him and seize the island. In the first part of this discussion Ariel mimics Trinculo's voice three times, simply calling out 'Thou liest', the third time earning the jester a beating from his friend.

When Caliban is allowed an uninterrupted explanation of what to do he emphasizes the burning of Prospero's books and the acquisition of Miranda as 'queen'. This passage is spoken by Caliban in verse which, as their drunken catch is silenced by mysterious music, played by the invisible Ariel, rises into sheer poetry giving lyrical emphasis to the strains which merely bemuse the other two. Would these be the spirits, described by Caliban as hostile to their human tyrant, communicating with their earthbound brother?

## *Commentary*

To the sweet concord of the last scene succeeds the foolish discord between savage and clown. Though thoroughly intoxicated, Caliban is developing as a character: he appears fully aware of his situation, of Prospero's usurpation and of the beauty of the magician's daughter; he resents Trinculo's scornful remarks; he concentrates already on what is for him the essence of all this foolery, twice muttering that they must *destroy* Prospero.

**Tell not me** i.e. don't tell me to stop all this drinking.
**bear up, and board 'em** Steer in a given direction and board the enemy ship (the bottle).
**They say** i.e. what has been told him, probably by Caliban between scenes, as Miranda is not mentioned till line 97.
**set** Fixed in a stare.
**brave** Fine.
**in his tail** Possibly an allusion to the peacock.
**My man-monster** My servant-monster.
**standard** Standard-bearer (though Caliban can scarcely 'stand').
**run** i.e. run away.
**go** Walk.
**say nothing** Be incapable of speech. Pun on 'lie'.
**in case** In a frame of mind.
**debosh'd** Debauched.
**natural** i.e. natural fool.
**supplant** Uproot.
**this thing** i.e. Trinculo.
**Thou shalt be lord of it** Caliban would exchange one master for another.
**compass'd** Brought about.

**party** Person concerned. Stephano affects a magisterial manner.
**I'll yield him ... head** A possible allusion to Jael and Sisera in Judges, iv,21.
**pied ninny** Parti-coloured fool. This reference (like 'patch' in the same line) to the motley dress of Trinculo is from something outside the experience of this island savage; 'ninny' (simpleton) is a possible corruption of 'innocent'.
**quick freshes** Fresh-water springs.
**stock-fish** Dried fish beaten before boiling.
**As you like this ... time** i.e. if this is the way you want it, call me a liar again. The accusation of lying has been transferred from Caliban to Stefano.
**and hearing too?** Deaf as well?
**murrain** A cattle disease, used in swearing, like 'a plague on'.
**stand further off** Addressed to Trinculo, to prevent further interference.
**paunch** Pierce his paunch (stomach).
**wezand** Wind-pipe.
**sot** Blockhead. Later associated with drink.
**brave brood** His own instincts, as expressed in I, 2, 352.
**plot** Outline of a play, especially a masque. Pun on 'conspiracy'.
**troll** Sing in full volume.
**catch** Song for several voices, each joining in in succession at the end of a line.
**While-ere** A short while ago.
**do reason** Do anything within reason.
**That's not the tune** Caliban remembers a song they have previously sung and recognizes that Ariel's tune is different.
**Art thou afeard?** Caliban's faith in his new master is shaken.
**twangling** Compound of 'twang' and 'jingle'.
**I remember the story** i.e. I have not forgotten the plot.
**taborer** Player on a tabor, a small drum accompanying a pipe.

## Act III Scene 3

Desperation is now the mood of the Neapolitans: the faithful old Gonzalo is too physically exhausted to go any farther; the King gives up any remaining hope of finding his son; the frustrated assassins grimly decide on a night operation. At this moment of general depression Prospero's spirits (grotesque but friendly shapes) wheel in a 'banquet' and withdraw. At first amazed and then philosophically prepared to believe everything ever told by travellers, they are about to eat when Ariel (dressed this time as a 'harpy') removes the untouched meal and addresses the three guilty men, who draw their swords in vain. Their past crime is made clear to them and the punishment shown as having overtaken them. True repentance alone will now save them from further harassment.

Ariel vanishes in thunder and the eerie attendants return to take away the table itself (appropriate perhaps after a magic entertainment). Praising Ariel and the lesser spirits, Prospero leaves his post of observation to visit his prisoner.

Alonso, who has only heard the message, transmitted, as he thinks, by winds and waves, while the thunder echoed the name 'Prospero', rushes off to join his son at the bottom of the sea, followed by the two villains, prepared to take on other 'devils'. The rest of the court, at the bidding of Gonzalo (who has recollections of past villainy), follow to prevent acts of sheer desperation.

## *Commentary*

Introduced into this scene of ugly reality in the form of death by drowning and carefully planned murder is what Sebastian calls a 'living drollery', a puppet-show of typical masque-like 'shapes', manipulated – much, indeed, as the human actors have been manipulated – by Prospero and his servant-spirits. We are entertained not so much by a dramatic rendering of an episode of actual life as by a device, quite an extravagant one, as artificial as an ornamental fountain – and as unnecssary! Whether Prospero's intention was to make the pangs of stimulated hunger sharpen the sense of torments present and future in the three accused is not clear; some critics treat the strange antics of the 'islanders' as an anti-masque preceding the main (and dignified) masque of goddesses in the next act.

Throughout Act II Prospero has been absent; in Act III he is the spectator-contriver backstage or aloft in the wings, watching Ariel perform his commands or speak his condemnations. The essence of the play is captured in this scene, when Prospero deputes to Ariel the lengthy pronunciation of judgment, reserving for himself the later speeches of forgiveness and reconciliation. Ariel, having just played Nobody's music to distract the three comic conspirators, here penetrates the consciences of the three greater villains, the blank verse rhythms echoing the sounds of waves and winds and distant thunder in the ears of the guilty.

**By'r lakin**  By Our Ladykin (the Virgin Mary).
**maze**  Labyrinth. The Hampton Court maze, the first in England, had been made in 1608.
**forth-rights and meanders**  Straight tracks and winding paths.
**attach'd**  Arrested (like a prisoner).
**one repulse**  i.e. when surprised by Gonzalo's awakening in II, 1.
**banquet**  In those days a light repast of fruit, sweetmeats and wine, taken usually some time after the main meal.
**kind keepers**  Guardian angels.
**living drollery**  Live puppet-show.
**unicorns**  Legendary animals with horses' bodies and a single straight horn projecting from their foreheads, sometimes associated with lions as supporters of the royal arms.
**phoenix**  A fabulous bird, the only one of its kind, that after some hundreds of years burnt itself to ashes, from which there grew each time a new one.
**what does else want credit**  What else is not to be believed.
**travellers ne'er did lie**  i.e. all travellers' tales are true.
**If I should say**  Lines 29–34 are an incomplete sentence.
**than of . . . any**  The structure has collapsed: it probably means, 'than our human species, of whom not many, nay hardly one, can compare with them.'
**muse**  Wonder at.
**Praise in departing**  i.e. keep your praise till the end. Is he thinking of the long speech to be made by Ariel?
**Dew-lapp'd like bulls**  i.e. goitre.
**Wallets**  Probably metathesis for 'wattles', fleshy protruberances from the necks of turkeys.
**whose heads . . . breasts**  Another 'traveller's tale', probably based on some local deformity.
**putter-out of five for one**  Traveller to dangerous parts. The custom was to deposit a sum of money, forfeited in the case of failure to return, but multiplied by five if the traveller came back.
**Good warrant of**  Sound proof of (the existence of these creatures).
**stand to**  Take my place in readiness.
**my last**  i.e. my last meal (should the food be poisonous).
**The best is past**  i.e. with the passing of my son.
**Brother, my lord the duke**  These two have remained apart, watching for an advantage.
*like a Harpy*  Again for Prospero's gratification, as the King and his companions cannot see Ariel. The classical harpy was a winged monster with the face of a woman and the body of a vulture with sharp claws. The three harpies fouled whatever they swooped on. In one legend they tormented their victim by carrying off every meal placed before him. In this masque-like episode the banquet vanishes by means of a 'quaint device' (ingenious arrangement).
**You are three men of sin**  Addressed only to the guilty; Gonzalo and company do not hear any words.

Act III Scene 3   49

**to instrument**   As an instrument.
**the never-surfeited sea**   The sea which can never drown too many (for its capacity). It is the object of 'hath caus'd', while 'Destiny' is the subject.
**where man doth not inhabit**   Prospero's sojourn is only an interruption of its generally uninhabited state.
**you 'mongst men ... to live**   i.e. you being fit to live only in a desert island.
**with such-like valour**   i.e. demented.
**Their proper selves**   Their own selves.
**the elements**   Better in apposition to 'ministers' and understood as the four elements which share in the 'tempering' of swords: earth, fire, water and air. Such elements cannot be said to wound the air or stab at water, so there must be an elided subject 'you' to be restored before 'may as well'.
**still-closing**   Always filling up again.
**diminish**   Make smaller (something in itself quite small).
**One dowle ... my plume**   One downy part of my crest of feathers.
**like**   Equally.
**massy**   Because their arms are paralysed.
**will not be**   Refuse to be.
**requit it**   Avenged the crime (in the shipwreck).
**delaying**   i.e. over the space of twelve years.
**all the creatures**   Such as the strange island spirits.
**ling'ring perdition**   A slow death.
**at once**   i.e. when it comes suddenly.
**step by step**   i.e. lingering.
**falls**   Singular verb to plural 'wraths'.
**is nothing**   i.e. there is nothing (to guard you).
**heart-sorrow**   Repentance.
**clear life ensuing**   Blameless life to follow.
*mocks and mows*   Grins and grimaces.
**devouring**   Better 'overwhelming' (in its gracefulness) than 'in the act of demolishing a banquet'.
**with good life ... strange**   In a lifelike manner and with rare (unusually accurate) observation.
**Their several kinds have done**   i.e. each has acted according to his 'kind'.
**knit up ... distractions**   As if transfixed in their distraught state.
**the billows**   Ariel was invisible.
**bass my trespass**   Tell me of my sin in a deep voice. Could Ariel have uttered these thunderous sounds?
**ooze**   Sea-bed.
**plummet**   Plumb-line, to find the depth of water under the keel.
**a great time after**   The passage of the twelve years.
**of suppler joints**   i.e. younger.
**ecstasy**   Madness.

## Revision questions on Act III

1 How many supernatural factors enter into this act?

2 What qualities in Miranda make her appeal to an audience?

3 What elements of (a) tragedy, (b) comedy, (c) poetry do you notice in Caliban during this act?

4 Do you think there is a subordinate climax in this act? Give your reasons for agreeing or disagreeing.

## Act IV Scene 1

Prospero explains his previous harsh treatment of Ferdinand as a testing of the genuineness of the latter's love for Miranda. Prospero has already agreed to the match, but once more (for the benefit of the audience) gives his formal approval and praises her virtues. After promising not to anticipate the marriage ceremony, Ferdinand is invited to sit and talk with Miranda (apart). Prospero then summons Ariel, gives him instructions for the entertainment to follow, and uses the interval to impress again on Ferdinand (so used to the intrigues of court life) the need to respect the innocence of his bride-to-be.

To the sound of music Iris (rainbow messenger of Juno, queen of the gods) calls on Ceres (goddess of agriculture) to appear and greet the approaching Juno. Ceres arrives and is told of the occasion, the celebration of a marriage contract. As the mother of Persephone (seized as a bride by Pluto), Ceres enquires if Venus (an accomplice in the seizure) is to make one of the company; Iris assures her that the goddess of love and her son, Cupid, are returning post-haste to their haunts after being frustrated in their attempts to seduce the young couple. Juno then enters and joins with Ceres in bestowing in song every possible happiness on Ferdinand and Miranda.

Ferdinand is overwhelmed by the spectacle and by the supernatural powers of his future father-in-law. As commanded by the two goddesses, Iris calls first on water-nymphs and then on reapers to leave their respective occupations and join in a dance. Before the finish, Prospero recollects the conspiracy of Caliban and his newly found associates and dismisses the performers so abruptly that he hastens to explain that the now vanished apparitions are as insubstantial as human life.

Ushering Ferdinand and Miranda into his grotto, he turns to Ariel for an account of the progress of the comic plotters. A graphic description of their misfortunes (into which they have been inveigled by Ariel's music) precedes their appearance, thoroughly pickled in alcohol and ditchwater. Caliban is being blamed by the others for their sad state when they catch sight of some gay garments strung out on a line to tempt them from their purpose. In vain Caliban scolds Stephano and Trinculo for their folly; after snatching all they can and loading Caliban with more, they are suddenly chased off-stage by spirits in the form of a pack of dogs, to face further torments, ordered by Prospero.

## *Commentary*

The last two acts are single scenes, both taking place on the very same spot, outside Prospero's grotto; indeed, the magician ends Act IV by leading Ariel out for some fresh instructions and opens Act V by returning attired in his magic robe. To this wide open space are summoned goddesses in person, a chorus of (immortal) nymphs and (mortal) reapers, and finally the befuddled rebels whom Caliban cannot stop from ruining their scheme. The same area has to accommodate all the characters in Act V's grand finale.

The opening and closing lines of Act IV are concerned with 'punishment', in one form to test future loyalty, in the other as retribution for past disloyalty. In these inflictions we recognize the severe moral code of Prospero: the sharp admonition of a court-bred prince and the continued chastisement of a savage for his attempt on Miranda. That this special anxiety for his daughter's virginity should be so emphatically presented may well be due to what Shakespeare had heard or read of 'scandalous' behaviour by some of the early colonists in Virginia. Reports of inexcusable idleness may also have suggested hard physical labour as a necessity on a remote island (see *Setting*). The 'test' referred to in 1.7 is of patient submission to seemingly endless toil devoted to a desirable goal, in this case the love of a maiden.

Such a 'masque' as this short episode of the three goddesses had become fashionable at contemporary noble weddings. That the whole play may have been adapted for such an occasion

## 52 The Tempest

would explain some of the oddities in this scene, chiefly the entry of three stately deities instead of what might have been expected of Ariel's 'rabble' with their 'mop and mow'. Temporary alterations may have been overlooked in the final version.

Although a magician (unable indeed to enforce loyalty but capable of preventing violence), Prospero uses a very commonplace device to frustrate the attempt on his life. In a play in which dress – Prospero's robe and his ducal outfit, Ariel's disguises, Caliban's gaberdine, and the courtiers' clothes unsullied by the sea-water – has considerable significance, a mere row of flashy garments on a clothes-line is sufficient to foil the trio. It is almost as if, in the role of Providence, Prospero allows Free Will in his world of magic to play a decisive part in bringing on catastrophe! It is of course more entertaining than some form of direct intervention would have been.

Prospero derives some self-satisfaction from his 'wonders', but there is not much of the serenity of the master conjuror. His irritability is perhaps that of an old man (forgetful at times) confined to an empty island and deprived of the exercise of his natural authority for twelve years. By turns he lectures, warns, reproves, praises, summons peremptorily and dismisses abruptly. His somewhat crabbed manner, however, will suddenly be exalted into the height of poetry. His recollection of Caliban and his knife leads to an old man's lengthy dissertation on the theme of all life being as transitory as a dream – this, while Caliban creeps ever nearer. Its sublimity of utterance anticipates the elaborate farewell to his art in the next act.

Among Ariel's tasks was the learning by heart of the speech of Ceres, a piece of homework the like of which would never again be imposed on him after his release!

**Your compensation makes amends** i.e. my repayment to you (the betrothal indicated in ll. 3–5) cancels out what you have suffered.
**third** i.e. as his only child.
**who** This subject pronoun becomes by an inversion the object.
**strangely** Rarely.
**halt** Limp.
**Against an oracle** Even if an oracle were to prophesy the opposite.
**purchas'd** Obtained.
**virgin-knot** A reference to the bride's maiden girdle at a Roman wedding.

Act IV Scene 1 53

**sanctimonious** Holy (without today's sarcastic overtones).
**aspersion** Sprinkling (a sign of heavenly grace).
**take heed... light you** Take care that you are properly wedded. Hymen, god of marriage, was usually represented with a torch (cf. line 97).
**fair issue** i.e. a healthy family.
**as 'tis now** i.e. as pure as it is at this moment.
**most opportune place** Locality most suited to temptation.
**Our worser genius can** i.e. our bad angel is capable of making. The Roman 'genius' originally meant each person's presiding spirit.
**or... Or** Either... or. The day will seem endlessly beautiful, because (1) the sun's career across the sky is halted by a mechanical breakdown, or (2) darkness has been held up by the arrest of Night below the horizon. Horses drew the chariot of the sun-god; Night was a classical goddess.
**your last service** i.e. the vanishing banquet.
**another trick** Similar device.
**rabble** Referring to the 'meaner fellows', though not contemptuous.
**some vanity** A trifling demonstration.
**with a twink** i.e. in the time taken to wink an eye.
**conceive** Understand.
**the strongest oaths** Like the three superlatives just used by Ferdinand.
**Abates the ardour of my liver** Prospero's typically stern reiteration draws from the prince an extreme conceit: the purity of his heart's thoughts subdues any sexual excitement (then associated with the liver).
**a corollary** One extra (modern 'supernumerary').
**want a spirit** i.e. be short of one performer.
**pertly** Smartly.
**be silent** Repetition of 'no tongue': speech would break the charm (line 127).
**Iris** Personification of the rainbow and special messenger of Juno.
**Ceres** Goddess of agriculture.
**leas** Meadows. Strictly arable fields grass-grown for pasture.
**turfy mountains** Grassy hillsides.
**thatch'd with stover** Covered with hay (with reference to its use as winter food).
**with pioned and twilled brims** The likeliest solution to this textual problem is 'with marsh-marigolds (peonies) and rushes at their brink'.
**spongy** Moisture-laden.
**at thy hest** At thy command.
**betrims** Makes gay (with their flowers).
**chaste crowns** Garlands for chaste nymphs.
**lass-lorn** Having lost his lass (old past participle of 'lose').
**poll-clipt** i.e. pruned by 'polling' or lopping or by removing the 'poll' or head.
**thyself dost air** Dost take the air.

## 54 The Tempest

**queen o' th' sky** Juno, wife of Jupiter, Roman king of the gods.
**wat'ry arch** i.e. the rainbow.
**her peacocks fly amain** i.e. the peacocks drawing her chariot are flying at top speed.
**to entertain** i.e. in preparation for Juno's arrival, at l. 102. The stage direction 'Juno descends' at 1.72 must be a printer's error.
**many-colour'd messenger** Referring to Iris's rainbow, of which blue is the dominant colour (1.80).
**saffron wings** The orange hue of the rainbow.
**honey-drops** The rain-drops against which the rainbow is formed.
**bosky** Wooded. Contrasted with the treeless down.
**Rich scarf** i.e. multi-coloured ribbon.
**short-grass'd green** Kept so by 'nibbling sheep'. But there are no signs of sheep on *this* island.
**estate** Bestow.
**Venus** Goddess of love; Cupid was her son.
**dusky Dis** Pluto, dark-skinned god of the underworld.
**my daughter** The beautiful Persephone, kidnapped by Pluto and by Jupiter's decision allowed six months of each year back on earth with her mother.
**scandal'd** Scandalous. Cupid had many amours.
**Of her society . . . afraid** You need not be afraid that she will be here.
**her deity** Cf. 'her ladyship'.
**Paphos** In Cyprus. One of the chief centres of the worship of Venus.
**Dove-drawn** The chariot of Venus was drawn by doves. This would be a return journey from the island after the failure in ll. 97–101.
**Some wanton charm** Against which Prospero had warned Ferdinand.
**Till Hymen's . . . be lighted** i.e. until the day of the wedding.
**Mars's hot minion** Venus had a love intrigue with Mars, Roman god of war.
**waspish-headed** Irritable.
**I know her by her gait** As a sister she should do! Perhaps this refers to Juno's majesty as a queen.
**Long continuance** i.e. many years.
**increasing** i.e. more of them.
**Hourly joys be still upon you** May transitory pleasures stay with you.
**foison plenty** Tautology, as in II, 1, 159. Another example is 'Scarcity and want' in 1.116.
**garners** Granaries.
**burthen** i.e. weight of fruit.
**Spring come to you . . . farthest** i.e. may the season of springtime be prolonged to its limit.
**charmingly** Referring to the sweetness of the singing and perhaps (as expressed in the following question) diagnosing enchantment.
**confines** Regions.
**wonder'd** Able to work wonders.
**Sweet** Miranda is about to speak.

Act IV Scene 1  55

**Naiads** Freshwater nymphs.
**windring** A remarkable printer's error, combining 'winding' and 'wandering'.
**sedg'd crowns** Chaplets of sedge, a rush-like plant.
**crisp channels** Water-courses with crinkled surfaces, caused by ripples.
**temperate** Chaste (consonant with the ceremony).
**sicklemen** i.e. reapers employing sickles.
**rye-straw** Suited to plaiting.
**footing** Dancing.
**heavily** Opposite of 'light-heartedly' (disappointment at not finishing the performance?).
**avoid** Away with you.
**so distemper'd** In such a bad mood.
**You do look... dismay'd** You look, such is your state of emotion, as if you had been disheartened by something.
**revels** The Master of the Revels was an English court official. Cf. Philostrate in *A Midsummer Night's Dream*, of whom Theseus asks 'What revels are in hand?'
**foretold you** Told you beforehand.
**thin air** The repetition emphasizes the insubstantiality of this element.
**baseless fabric** i.e. structure not built on solid foundations.
**all which it inherit** All those who live on it.
**like this insubstantial pageant faded** Like this spectacle conjured out of the air, which you have just beheld. This comparison repeats that of 1.151 in different words.
**rack** Cloud fragment in the wake of a storm.
**We** i.e. human beings, following up 1.154.
**rounded** Finished off.
**vex'd** Agitated (no longer angry).
**disturb'd with my infirmity** Upset over my weakness.
**If you be pleas'd** Curiously formal, like 'We wish you peace.'
**beating** Throbbing (with anger or confusion?).
**I thank thee** To Ariel, in anticipation.
**cleave to** Follow closely.
**presented** Acted the part of.
**Lest I might anger thee** i.e. by interrupting the masque.
**Say again... I told you, sir** This must refer to previous information given by Ariel to Prospero, after he had corralled the three in a pond in order to find time to play Ceres. It is repeated for the benefit of the audience.
**always bending... project** Making undeterred for the place where their plan was to be carried out.
**unback'd** Not broken in.
**Advanc'd their eyelids** Raised their eyes. Cf. I, 2, 411.
**As** As if. The act of enjoying a smell is more conspicuous than that of listening to music.

**calf-like** i.e. tamely following my pipe (it may be presumed Ariel is using this as well as his tabor), as a calf keeps to the trail of its lowing mother.

**goss** Gorse.

**filthy-mantled** With scum on the surface.

**O'erstunk** Stank worse than their feet normally did.

**trumpery** Trash (cf. 1. 224). Expressing contempt for the cheap but flashy objects that would tempt the primitive tastes of savages.

**stale** Decoy.

**Nurture** Training. The contrast is emphasized by the similarity of sound.

**Humanely** Out of kindness.

**blind mole** i.e. with its acute hearing.

**harmless fairy** Cf. III, 2, 134. Stephano uses the popular word for Prospero's spirits.

**played the Jack with** Tricked (1) like a knave, or (2) like a Jack o' Lantern (will o' the wisp).

**hoodwink** Blot out, as with a hood. From blindfolding a hawk during its training.

**fetch off ... o'er ears** i.e. rescue my bottle if I have to dive for it.

**O King Stephano! O peer!** Linking the butler's name with a popular ballad, sung by Iago in *Othello* (II, 3, 92) and in 1765 printed in Percy's *Reliques of Ancient Poetry*. The first stanza runs:

King Stephen was a worthy peere,
 His breeches cost him but a crowne,
He held them sixpence all too deere;
 Therefore he called the taylor Lowne.

**frippery** Old clothes shop.

**dropsy** Watery swellings in the human body.

**this fool** Either (1) idiot, or (2) clown.

**luggage** In contemporary use as baggage that is a hindrance to movement.

**jerkin** A short coat.

**under the line** (1) He has taken the jerkin off the clothes line and (2) below the Equator. At the time it was believed that diseases contracted in that region left men bald. An obscure joke.

**by line and level** i.e. accurately.

**an't like your grace** If it please your majesty.

**pass of pate** lit. thrust with the head, i.e. stroke of wit.

**lime** Bird-lime is sticky.

**barnacles** Wild geese, once supposed to be produced from the shell-fish of that name.

**Mountain ... Silver ... Fury ... Tyrant** Such names convey the impression of an English pack of hounds. One must not cavil that these visitants from the spirit world should be identifiable individually as if they were permanently kennelled on the island!

**dry convulsions** Caused by the absence of fluid in the joints.

**aged cramps** Cramps that afflict the aged.
**pinch-spotted** Covered with the marks of pinches as numerous as spots on a 'pard' (leopard).
**cat-o'-mountain** Wild cat.

### Revision questions on Act IV

1 Are any flaws in Prospero's character shown up in this act?

2 How does the masque celebrate 'a contract of true love'? Comment on the use of such material in this play.

3 Is this act best regarded as one scene?

### Act V Scene 1

Prospero reappears in his robe, attended by Ariel, who has a busy time ahead of him before his release from servitude. The lonely magician takes pleasure in the approaching climax of his 'project' (a multiple one); he has inflicted remorse on the three guilty men in much the same way as he has tormented Caliban and his associates with cramps. However, Ariel's plea for mercy leads him, after drawing a comparison between his supposedly human feelings and those of a mere sprite, to forgive his enemies. While his messenger is away releasing the prisoners (as we now know them to be) Prospero apostrophizes the unseen powers with whose aid he has brought about incredible natural phenomena and announces his intention – a secret between him and the audience beyond the footlights – to surrender his magic powers, putting his staff and book out of reach of any would-be successor.

His last performance is the musical spell he casts upon the Neapolitans, who arrive in the distraught condition in which they left the stage in III, 3, the desperate Alonso attended by a tearful Gonzalo, the other two by Adrian and Francisco. Prospero addresses them in words that speak to the consciences of the principals in turn (and to them alone). Assisted by Ariel he discards his robe and becomes visible to them, dressed as he was when Duke of Milan, complete with hat and rapier. While Ariel speeds to the ship to bring ashore the master and boatswain (last met in the opening scene) the courtiers gradually recover their senses though, after their recent experiences, they fear this figure of the former duke may be yet another piece of conjuring. Alonso, however, is reassured and forgiven, Sebastian and Antonio privately threatened – and forgiven – and then the ugly past is supplanted by the enchanting future. Playing on the word 'lost' as applied first to the King's son and then to his own daughter, Prospero makes a reality (by natural means this time) of the vision that has just occurred to Alonso – the union of two young people whom he thought dead. Prospero draws back a curtain and reveals that they are alive, immersed in chess and very much in love. Ferdinand is overjoyed to find his father has not been drowned, Miranda overcome by the sight of so many fine humans (a touch of dramatic irony).

Fittingly the now fully recovered Gonzalo pronounces a comprehensive blessing on the happy pair; it is he, too, who recognizes the gallows-bird of a boatswain when the two mariners are led in by Ariel; again, the boatswain is the spokesman, doing full justice to the wonders that have happened to the ship and its crew. Alonso is being promised a detailed explanation later on of all these marvels when there is a further irruption, as Ariel drives in the two dishevelled retainers and a disillusioned and repentant Caliban. Note how the two conspirators recover a measure of self-respect by teasing these unfortunates, while Prospero reverts to his earlier severity to punish them for their intended assault on his life by having them tidy up his grotto (in preparation for the accommodation, in rather limited quarters, of the King and his court). The next day they will set sail for Naples to celebrate the marriage, their safety at sea being Ariel's last task.

In *A Midsummer Night's Dream* the plea to the audience in the Epilogue is spoken by the fairy Puck; in *The Tempest* a similar appeal is made, not by the spirit Ariel, but by his magician master. This, taken with the speeches 'These our actors' . . .' in Act IV and 'Ye elves of hills . . .' in this Act, has led generations to imagine the actor-author bidding farewell to his contemporaries when about to make his own return journey to Stratford, in Warwickshire.

### Commentary

It is Gonzalo ('holy' in *character*) who, having emerged from a state of puzzlement and tears, gives the clearest and most succinct definition of Prospero's 'project', in ll. 208–12; he ascribes

Act V Scene 1  59

the whole scheme to the gods (remember that the word 'God' was forbidden on the Stuart stage), to which claim Alonso adds a pious 'Amen'.

The King's persistent questioning, 'Give us particulars', 'say how thou cam'st here', 'how came you hither?' underlines the marvellous in what has been happening and indicates the growing uneasiness of a practical mind: 'there is in this business more than nature Was ever conduct of'. His two servants dead drunk on a desert island and keeping company with a monstrous-looking savage are sufficient cause for wonder, but behind the series of supernatural incidents lies a mystery to which he seeks a solution, if need be from an oracle. The oracle is at hand and the play ends with Prospero's promise to account for everything (or nearly everything), just as it began with his long delayed explanation to his daughter in I, 2. One wonders how Alonso reacted that evening to the 'wonders' staged by his son's new father-in-law.

Himself the victim of the abuse of political power, Prospero is spared to combine the theoretical magic learnt from his book with the practical forces of the supernatural in the island, a result of his freeing Ariel from the tree-trunk. Thus securing the services of this dainty sprite, who has been assisted by other fairies and goblins, he has worked the miracles so eloquently described in his farewell speech — mostly it would seem rehearsals for the terrifying storm which puts his enemies within his power. The nature of his project makes it that the climax is towards the end of the play, using the word in the popular sense of the highest point; this might well be the lines 106–11:

> Behold, sir King,
> The wronged Duke of Milan, Prospero ...
> ... to thee and thy company I bid
> A hearty welcome.

Over half the lines of this Act are spoken by the wronged duke: he gloats, relents, soliloquizes, praises publicly, condemns secretly, ridicules and reflects on his own advancing years. He *listens*, too, to Ariel's expressed sympathy for the sufferings of the guilty, to Alonso's inconsolable grief, to Gonzalo's unquenched enthusiasm for a happy outcome, to the boatswain's sober account of a mariner's miracle, to Caliban's sullen resentment at being duped. He promises his new circle of friends an evening's entertainment with the quite spell-binding narrative of 'My exile from Milan'.

In this act Ariel is on his own, here, there and everywhere,

60 The Tempest

carrying out his master's commands while the latter makes his speeches of denunciation and reconciliation; he leads onto the stage three distinct groups of characters, valets Prospero and finally ensures a safe passage for all to Naples; this potent elemental spirit can nevertheless imagine human feelings, he has his eye on the clock, and he pants for freedom, not in any 'cloud-capp'd towers' but:

Under the blossom that hangs on the bough.

**crack not**  i.e. do no fail (under the strain).
**Goes upright with his carriage**  Does not bend under the weight of what he is carrying.
**at which time ... should cease**  The whole action of the play is contained within 24 hours.
**I did say so**  Events like Caliban's conspiracy have since delayed the project.
**gave in charge**  Ordered.
**the line-grove**  This must be *lime*-trees in a short avenue (line); in IV, 1, 193 Prospero would hardly have singled out one tree. Perhaps (a rather humdrum result of much research) the clothes-*line* was suspended between two *limes*).
**weather-fends**  Protects from the weather.
**till your release**  Until you release them.
**from eaves of reeds**  i.e. dripping separately from the ends of the reeds in a thatched roof.
**your affections ... tender**  Ariel now displays feelings appropriate to a human; he acts as a catalyst to the accumulated anger of his master.
**One of their kind**  i.e. human, like Alonso.
**that relish all as sharply**  Who (i.e. Prospero) react to every sensation as keenly as they do.
**Passion as they**  (Who) feel as deeply as they do. The main verb is 'shall not (myself) be mov'd'.
**kindlier mov'd**  i.e. stirred by more human (and therefore kinder) emotions (than those of a spirit).
**high wrongs**  Grave injuries.
**struck to th' quick**  Deeply and sorely hurt. The 'quick' is any sensitive part of a living body.
**nobler**  i.e. in comparison with blind anger.
**the rarer action is ... vengeance**  i.e. it is rarer to act virtuously than to take one's revenge.
**further**  i.e. than accepting such penitence.
**Ye elves of hills ...**  The resemblance of these lines to the following passage in Golding's translation of Medea's speech in Ovid's *Metamorphoses* (1567) is remarkable:
   Ye Ayres and windes; ye Elues of Hills, of Brookes, of Woods alone,
   Of standing Lakes and of the Night, approche ye euerychone.

Through helpe of whom (the crooked bankes much wondring at the thing)
I have compelled streames to run cleane backward to their spring.
By charmes I make the calme Seas rough, and make the rough Seas playne,
And couer all the Skie with Cloudes and chase them thence againe.
By charmes I raise and lay the windes, and burst the Vipers jaw,
And from the bowels of the Earth both stones and trees doe draw.
Whole woods and Forestes I remoue; I make the Mountaines shake,
And euen the Earth it selfe to grone and fearefully to quake.
I call up dead men from their graves; and thee, O lightsome Moone
I darken oft, though beaten brasse abate thy perill soone.
Our Sorcerie dimmes the Morning faire, and darkes the Sun at Noone.
The flaming breath of fierie Bulles ye quenched for my sake
And caused their unwieldie neckes the bended yoke to take.
Among the Earthbred brothers you a mortall warre did set
And brought a sleepe the Dragon fell whose eyes were never shet.

**printless foot** The spirits leave no visible mark.
**Neptune** The sea.
**demi-puppets** (Small) fairies.
**ringlets** 'Fairy rings' of richer grass, caused by fungi.
**that rejoice ... curfew** Who welcome the onset of darkness.
**weak masters** Spirits of limited power.
**mutinous** Classical epithet for winds, where we now use 'turbulent', itself derived from the Latin *turba*, a disorderly mob.
**azur'd** Past participle for the plain adjective, as if laid on with paint. This occurs mostly with colours.
**war** Cf. Miranda's opening lines, I, 2, 3–5.
**dread rattling** Instilling fear by its loud rattle.
**fire** i.e. the lightning flash.
**rifted Jove's ... bolt** Cloven the oak (sacred to Jupiter) with the thunderbolt (Jupiter's special weapon).
**strong-bas'd promontory** Headland on firm enough foundations to resist erosion by the waves.
**spurs** Roots (those above ground).
**graves at my command ... forth** This 'wonder' can be accepted with the rest if we consider the whole passage as symbolizing Shakespeare's farewell to his career as a playwright; or it may have been simply taken over from Golding (see above).
**To work mine end ... senses** i.e. to make them realize the purpose of my project.
**that This airy charm is for** For which purpose this invisible spell is being laid upon them.
**the best comforter ... fancy** The best way to soothe a disordered imagination.
**boil'd within thy skull** This must be addressed to Alonso; 'you' in line

## 62 The Tempest

61 is addressed to the whole group. The expression suggests overheating by feverish anxiety.

**spell-stopp'd** Rendered motionless, as indicated in the stage direction 'stand charm'd'. There is a pause before Prospero turns to Gonzalo.

**Holy** In earlier sense of 'free from sin'.

**sociable to** In sympathy with.

**Fall fellowly drops** Let fall tears of comradeship.

**their rising senses ... clearer reason** i.e. their growing awareness is dispersing the mists of incomprehension that have clouded their minds, which are now able to think clearly. This observation is repeated in other words in ll. 79–82.

**To him thou follow'st** To Alonso.

**graces** Kindnesses.

**pinch'd for't now ... Flesh and blood** These are the pinches of conscience, unlike the physical ones inflicted on Caliban (see 'inward pinches' in line 77), unless 'flesh and blood' applies to Sebastian and refers to both kinds; but this phrase is so familiar in the sense of 'kindred' (and presumed fellow-feeling) that it must be Prospero's ironical apostrophe of Antonio, who shows no true kinship or consequent affection. Note that he uses the same indirect approach to Sebastian with 'Thy brother'.

**remorse** Pity.

**nature** i.e. in attacking a brother (see 'unnatural' in l.79).

**I do forgive thee** But would Alonso? Note the change to the familiar second singular from the severe '*You*, brother mine.'

**fill the reasonable shore** Metaphor for understanding flooding into minds once again capable of reasoning.

**Not one of them ... know me** Not one of them is so far looking at me (invisible in a magic robe), nor would he recognize me if he saw me.

**discase me** Take off my robe. Thereby appearing before the others as (helped by an invisible Ariel) he puts on his once familiar hat and rapier, adjusting them 'so, so, so'.

*After summer* In pursuit of summer.

**Being awake** Having been wakened (by you).

**Inhabits here** He means that the cause of these emotions – some magic power – occupies the island.

**some heavenly power** A substitute for the stage-banned 'God'.

**this fearful country** Far removed from his Utopian sketch in II, 1, 143.

**some enchanted trifle** He remembers the banquet.

**as of flesh and blood** As being a live human being.

**I'll not swear** Though Gonzalo beholds the very same duke he helped on a forlorn journey, he is reluctant to believe he is still alive.

**taste ... subtleties** Are subject to some magic influences (lit. 'delicacies from the kitchen').

**brace** Pair. Used of hounds or game-birds, it is here contemptuous.

**pluck** Draw down.

Act V, Scene 1  63

**No** This superfluous word could mean that Prospero has overheard Sebastian.
**all of them.** All thy faults. Antonio has nothing further to say until he loosens his tongue on poor Caliban. He is an ungracious 'penitent'.
**I am woe for't** A formal expression, as Prospero has no need to be 'woeful'.
**sovereign aid** Help efficacious above all others.
**As great to me, as late** i.e. both heavy and recent.
**supportable ... weaker** i.e. I have poorer resources (being only an exiled duke, or having no other child, as Alonso has) to render my sad loss more endurable.
**that they were** His wish is a touching case of dramatic irony, emphasized by repetition.
**In this last tempest** i.e. 'lost' to one 'lost' in the storm. No need for Prospero to elucidate this conundrum, as he has the visual answer close by.
**do so much admire** Are so full of wonder.
**they devour their reason** i.e. their reason is swallowed up in amazement.
**their words ... breath** (Scarce think) that their voices are their own.
**justled from** Driven out of (jostled).
**abroad** Beyond this cell.
**As much as me my dukedom** As much as my (restored) dukedom contents me.
**for a score of kingdoms ... wrangle** Should you, for something *less* than the world, dispute my charge.
**A vision** Another hallucination.
**merciful** i.e. in sparing his father.
**Your eld'st acquaintance** The longest knowledge you have had of each other.
**of whom I have ... second life** i.e. who has saved me from drowning.
**I am hers** i.e. I am now a second father to *her*.
**my child** i.e. Miranda.
**A heaviness that's gone** Past sorrow.
**Should have spoke ere this** The first time that Gonzalo has been at a loss for words.
**chalk'd forth** Marked out.
**his own** i.e. in his right mind.
**still embrace** Always afflict.
**blasphemy** Blasphemer.
**That swear'st grace o'er board** i.e. who filled the vessel with oaths.
**Hast thou no mouth?** The seamen are at first speechless.
**three glasses** Three hours.
**yare** Ready.
**all this service ... since I went** Ariel's last errand was only to waken these two and bring them to the grotto. The rest was reported done in I, 2, 226. Nevertheless this exaggeration meets with affectionate admiration (in the same line)!

## 64 The Tempest

**tricksy** Resourceful.
**dead of sleep** In a dead sleep.
**strange and several noises** Undoing the effects of the storm was as noisy as the storm itself, impressing the audience with Prospero's discarded powers.
**in all our trim** i.e. with our clothes fresh and not drenched.
**freshly** i.e. in a renovated condition. While the adverb strictly modifies 'beheld', the description seems shared between crew and ship.
**Cap'ring** Dancing for joy.
**on a trice** Instantly. Cf. the modern 'at a bound'.
**Even in a dream** The work of Ariel.
**moping** Feeling bewildered.
**diligence** Diligent spirit. For the figurative use of an abstract noun for a person, cf. 'blasphemy' l.218.
**conduct of** i.e. agent in producing.
**beating on** Puzzling over. Cf. IV, 1, 163.
**pick'd leisure** A chosen time.
**shortly single** Soon and in private.
**seem probable** i.e. be made convincing.
**of every** Of each of. Excluding of course the conspiracy.
**happen'd accidents** Things that really happened. Tautology in a dialogue distorted with elisions!
**Every man shift ... for himself** A drunken piece of philanthropy inverting the usual desperate cry when abandoning ship.
**bully-monster** Friend monster.
**spies** i.e. eyes.
**brave spirits** A comic parallel to Miranda's admiration.
**What things are these** The rebuked villains revert to their badinage.
**the badges** Perhaps some armorial devices on the garments (made in Milan) stolen from the line by Stephano and Trinculo.
**true** i.e. genuine members of the crew and not more of Prospero's creations.
**That could** That she could. Such powers were attributed to some witches.
**make flows and ebbs** i.e. have lunar influence on the tides.
**deal in her command** i.e. share the moon's authority without being physically capable of her activites.
**demi-devil** i.e. having a devil as his father.
**thing of darkness** i.e. of evil, not from the colour of his skin.
**Is not this Stephano** Rather belated recognition, implying what a dreadful state the butler is in.
**reeling ripe** Staggering with all the wine he has consumed.
**grand** Special brand of.
**gilded 'em** Made them so drunk.
**pickle** (1) plight, or (2) preservative (against maggots).
**cramp** i.e. a bundle of pains.
**disproportion'd** Awkward.

**trim it handsomely** Back to domestic service!
**seek for grace** Curry favour (with my master).
**this dull fool** This seems to refer to Trinculo, but Caliban was no worshipper of the clown.
**bestow your luggage** A curious command to come from a guest. And they found it at this very spot, in Act IV.
**Every third thought** i.e. the subject of frequent reflection.
**Take the ear strangely** i.e. absorb the attention of the listener. 'Strange' is about the commonest word in the King's vocabulary: cf. ll. 117, 228, 242, 289 and II, 1, 108.
**sail so expeditious ... catch** A voyage so speedy that you will overtake.
**draw near** Inviting the others into the grotto.

### *Epilogue*

***o'erthrown*** Thrown over.
***by you*** Both alternatives are open to the audience.
***hands ... breath*** i.e. clapping ... applause.
***want*** Lack.
***assaults Mercy itself*** Reaches the Mercy-Seat.
***frees*** Pardons.
***indulgence*** Toleration (of my faults).

## Revision questions on Act V

**1** How many people are taken by surprise in this act and what are the causes of their surprise?

**2** What does this act reveal of the relationship between Prospero and Ariel? Quote where you can.

**3** Give in your own words Prospero's description of his purpose and powers.

**4** What character changes do you notice during the course of Act V?

# Shakespeare's art in *The Tempest*

'Thou art not for an age but for all time.' (Ben Jonson)

## Introduction

Shakespeare achieved two firsts in our national literature, as poet and as playwright – something not claimed for any man of letters in any other nation. His plays have received worldwide recognition; his poetry is embedded in the dialogue of those plays. His powers of expression matched his genius in the creation of character. His lines, the best of which were poetically inspired, were composed for the utterance of professional actors entertaining audiences of varying tastes. He knew his fellow-actors and the roles they were best at undertaking. Through them as mouthpieces he was also at work on the minds of those who watched his dramas unfold, showing them human nature at its best and its worst, stimulating their imaginations by bringing old stories to life before their eyes and affording them opportunities to exercise their judgement between right and wrong, loyalty and treachery, love and hate, wisdom and folly. They beheld good and evil deeds, understood the motives and flinched at the consequences. All the world became a stage, and for the space of a dream the stage became a world in itself – ideal, not real, the shadow for the substance, a world of tricks and illusions in which a man is so easily imposed upon. For generations it has been argued that his marvellous inventions could not possibly be the work of a countryman come up to town; the mystery of his personality, on the other hand, reinforces the appeal of his creations.

He was many-sided, with no bias, no doctrine to preach, no malice towards his contemporaries, no subservience to authority and no respect for mobs; he sculpted life from the beautiful to the grotesque, without sentiment or cynicism. What personal feelings he had – attractions to friends and emotional involvements with women – he expressed in a few poems and sonnets which cannot be positively said to be either based on real experience or written merely as literary exercises. In brief, Shakespeare was a poetical dramatist, not a poet who used the forms of drama, as did our second greatest poet, John Milton. It is the poetry that enriches the study of his work away from the stage and endows his characters with the immortality of endless editions.

His greatness was acknowledged in his own day, and his works, while they fluctuated in public esteem during the following centuries, have never been more popular than during the past hundred years. Scholars in various parts of the world have devoted years, in some cases a lifetime, to wider and more intensive research into the texts, and to the discovery of fresh clues and new interpretations. In all but a few of his plays his imagination and wealth of diction have stirred the hearts of full houses – the voices may change, but the words are the same. None of his plays was written for the study: all had to come across the boards to that sea of faces on whose reception (handclaps or hisses) depended their success or failure. Least of all would their author have expected to be a staple topic for generations of students taking examinations in English Literature.

In the following commentary opinions are those formed or accepted by the editor; they are offered to the student as an aid to forming his own judgements and, it is hoped, getting more enjoyment from this play. Many admirers have seen in *The Tempest* Shakespeare in the light of the setting sun: was this his symbolic farewell to the stage, his actors and their audiences? The student should try to decide this matter for himself, avoiding some fashionable interpretations. He may well ask himself first, would Shakespeare really like to see himself in the severe, often ungracious character of the magician-duke (more closely resembling his often irritable sovereign)? If Naples be taken to represent Stratford-on-Avon, is it likely that the owner of New Place, whose slight regard for the citizenry is barely concealed in his works, would, even as a gesture, seek its permission to retire?

Certainly, in this final period, Shakespeare shows a growing detachment from his characters. The same skill is there, but the outline is less clear, the features not so well-defined. Perhaps, with every third thought being of the grave, he was more concerned with human destiny as a whole than with individual peculiarities, more intent to show that good may come of evil than that Caliban had a soul. In the composition of the dialogue and the management of plots (though here *The Tempest* is an exception) are signs of that carelessness which left his literary works to the mercy of chance and the charitable endeavours of the two fellow-players whose First Folio did not appear till 1623.

However, these uncertainties and incongruities (one wonders why Prospero's magic was powerless to repeal his banishment) are not noticed in a play which appeals to an audience by its striking contrasts between good and evil, innocence and guilt. It may have had topical value as a marriage piece or as a presentation of the native question or as a fantasia on statecraft, but its universal qualities, as in the greater part of Shakespeare's work, are unfailing in their effect. Its spectators, having by their indulgence set Prospero free, may well come away feeling more understanding, more tolerant, more forgiving.

# Structure, themes, setting

## Structure

Critics have remarked on the preservation, exceptional in Shakespeare, of *the unities of time and place* (the classic principle that a play should consist of one plot, happening at one time – certainly not more than a day – and in one place), in this play. They have suggested a half-humorous purpose in it, as if the dramatist intended to show how well he could obey the canon when he chose.

After the first scene, it is true, the action is confined to the island: there are only nine scenes in all. Prospero always appears before his cell, there to send Ariel on his errands; to receive his reports; or to draw to him, by the sound of the attendant spirit's music, first one, then another set of characters. On the other hand, four of the nine scenes are set 'in another part of the island' (all different), which is hardly unity of place in the classical sense.

Again, the short duration of the action (three hours to be exact; see V, 1, 223, where 'glasses' means hour-glasses, i.e. recording the passage of three hours) seems less an adherence to the unity of time than a consequence of the swift movements of Ariel, eager for his release (promised 'after two days' in I, 2, 298). The rapidity with which (1) the young couple's acquaintance matures, (2) the guilty three are made to repent and (3) Caliban's rebellion is crushed, quite simply conforms to the whole atmosphere of enchantment. In a magic island much may happen in the briefest space of time.

Indeed, Shakespeare's construction owes little to conventional laws, much to the continuity of cause and effect and to the blending of major and minor stories into one satisfying whole – irrespective of probability, the lapse of time, or preciseness of locality.

The action of the play is simple and in places symmetrical. The following parallels may be noted:

| | |
|---|---|
| Banishment of Prospero | Banishment of Sycorax |
| Conspiracy against Alonso | Conspiracy against Prospero |
| 'King' Gonzalo | 'King' Stephano |
| The dumb show | The masque |
| Prospero's absorption in magic studies | Alonso's absorption in his loss |

There are no strong dramatic situations; never is there any doubt of the issue. Prospero is, throughout, the master of the fate of the others.

## Themes

Though the first play in the First Folio, *The Tempest*, together with *Cymbeline* and *The Winter's Tale*, belongs to the last period of Shakespeare's dramatic career. Its diction alone would place it there, but it has in common with these other plays a high moral seriousness. The period of bitter tragedy is over and the serenity of one who has emerged from the dark casts sweetness and light over human relations. There is so strange an other-worldliness about these last plays – so different from the gay brilliance of the earlier ones – that they have been called 'Romances'.

The main theme of *The Tempest* would seem to be **forgiveness – after repentance**; yet Alonso's mood shortly before Prospero's revelations is rather one of mad despair induced by supernatural terrors than the true remorse of a guilty soul. Indeed, the wrong done is so far back that Alonso has to be reminded of it; and then it becomes to him just a reason for the loss that overwhelms him.

Prospero, in one sense the author of all that takes place on the stage, is rejoicing over the complete success of his 'project', when the remark let slip by Ariel that his heart would melt at the sight of the sufferers, *were he human*, brings him to the merciful decision that would appear to have been his ultimate goal throughout:

Though with their high wrongs I am struck to th' quick,
Yet with my nobler reason 'gainst my fury
Do I take part: the rarer action is
In virtue than in vengeance: they being penitent
The sole drift of my purpose doth extend
Not a frown further. (V, 1, 25–30)

## Structure, themes, setting 71

In these last plays shines the radiance of womanly perfection. Miranda is not a suffering heroine like Hermione and Imogen, nor is she lost and restored (except in the sense playfully adopted by Prospero), but she shares with Marina and Perdita the ethereal beauty of unspoilt maidenhood.

Typical, too, is the avoidance of a tragic ending; not only are the criminals and the blunderers prevented from committing murder – they are forgiven. All ends in peace and reconciliation, with music no mere accessory, as in the earlier comedies, but an active achievement of the action, in fact 'instrumental' in two different senses of the word. It intensifies, with its unseen singers and airy tunes, the atmosphere of enchantment.

There is another element in the play, familiar to us, but of novel interest to a Jacobean audience: what is still called the colonial problem. Already the native tribesman was being exploited by the white invader, attracted by the fertility of newly-discovered territories; slave labour and the hateful traffic in liquor have been transferred by Shakespeare from the West Indies to somewhere in the Mediterranean.

## Setting

The description of Prospero's island is unusually, perhaps purposely vague. Placed in the Mediterranean sea, somewhere off the route from Tunis to Naples, it has the drowsy atmosphere and tropical violence of the 'still-vex'd Bermoothes' in the West Indies. The few details we are given come from Prospero's apostrophe of the spirits behind the natural features (hills, trees, streams and lakes) and Caliban's more down-to-earth list of comestibles for a primitive existence (berries, crab-apples, ground-nuts, birds' eggs and young nestlings): to these may be added his persecution by hedgehogs and adders and the cross-country torment of briars and thorns, furze and gorse, ending in a stagnant pond. It is a very English setting, save only for the mention of apes and monkeys (marmosets), and the fear of wolves and bears. Perhaps Sebastian thought he was stranded in Africa when he pretended to hear the roar of lions. No 'part of the island' seems to be on the sea-shore, though Prospero pictures the flowing wave chasing the sprites whose flying feet have left no prints behind; the grotto has its view of the sea.

This nameless island is no ordinary one: at the magician's

bidding spirits assume various animal shapes or even human forms stranger than those reported by those who then rounded Cape Horn. Contemporary travellers' tales, indeed, made any stage-setting credible. The atmosphere of magic is still further heightened by the music from invisible instruments; true enough that much of Shakespeare's incidental music came from 'off-stage', but this is 'played by the picture of Nobody' and it drives Trinculo to repentance and Stephano to defiance of the devils come, as he thinks, to fetch him. But, like most 'savages', Caliban is so susceptible to strains of sweet music, vocal and instrumental, that, metrically measurable as his speech is nearly always, in one passage he rises to poetic heights. His name is probably a playful anagram by Shakespeare of the newly coined 'Can(n)ibal' from a warlike tribe of West Indians, whose name, Caribs, has been given to the Caribbean Sea, ringed with its islands.

It was in this new world that the term 'plantation' became so well-known. Settlements, like that in Virginia for which the expedition under Sir George Somers was destined, had mixed fortunes; some failures were due to something other than native hostility, which was limited: the settlers themselves were apt to be quarrelsome, bone-idle, self-indulgent and immoral. In contrast the Brethren maintained strict discipline, reflected probably in the sternness of Prospero's rebukes, his belief in hard work as a test of character and his solemn warning against sex before marriage.

The poetry that informs so much of Shakespeare's work is at its most imaginative in this imaginary island, where the real world seems remote. Yet the very freedom to create is a test of the dramatist's skill: he must not exceed the bounds of probability, even when working wonders of enchantment. The measure of his success is that the two creatures who differ from the rest in being, one a spirit and the other only half human, leave a stronger impression on the mind than the mere humans, Prospero excepted. The humans, quite a cross-section of society, return to a normal life on the mainland; the fairy and the monster are restored to their respective worlds.

Prospero's vision, expressed in 'These our actors ...' (IV,1,148ff.) should be compared with that of Theseus in *A Midsummer Night's Dream* (V,1,4–17) for the 'shapes' that are created by the poet's imagination out of nothing and which return to nothing. In the latter play human quarrels are fomented for the amusement of fairies; in this play the spirits are instrumental in redressing deep wrongs. They are, too, under the control of a human magician who, testy and humourless as any Puritanical island governor, here personifies that wisdom which puts virtue before vengeance and beholds the transitoriness of this world.

> We are such stuff
> As dreams are made on, and our little life
> Is rounded with a sleep. (IV, 1, 156–8)

Shakespeare's 'revels' may have ended, and the actors of his and later generations may have 'melted into air', but his island lives on in the world of the imagination with its sweet music and uncouth forms, its love at first sight and its ultimate reconciliations.

## The supernatural

The exercise of Prospero's magic powers began after his arrival on the island and is surrendered at his departure. It is, perhaps, the island that is enchanted rather than Prospero that is the enchanter. He had been preceded by the exiled witch Sycorax. Providence, not his 'art', had brought him to shore. Once there, however, he found the right conditions in which to try his skill. The freeing of Ariel on condition of serving him for a period (it proved to be twelve years) enabled him to assume control over the spirit world.

> It was mine Art,
> When I arriv'd and heard thee, that made gape
> The pine, and let thee out. (I, 2, 291–3)

The more prosaic may object that Prospero may have used nothing more sensational than an axe; but this does not explain Ariel's wholesome fear, elemental spirit as he is, of being once more imprisoned in a tree.

Compared with Ariel's lightning flashes and dockyard repairs, Prospero with his wand exerts a more limited, hypnotic influence, charming Miranda to sleep, disarming Ferdinand, and drawing a circle round King and courtiers. He casts spells, too, now tormenting the body of Caliban, now chastening the spirits of the malefactors.

When Prospero would work magic, he assumes his robe, so

investing himself in the eyes of the audience with all the authority of a magician; similarly the superhuman nature of Ariel is made manifest to the same audience by his ability to transform himself into a sea nymph or a harpy, so pleasing both his master and his master's masters, the spectators.

Whereas in other Shakespeare plays the supernatural, in the form of fairies, ghosts or weird sisters, intrudes upon the human world, here the human element makes a unique incursion into the supernatural world. The whole action of the play depends on the supernatural: there is no intensification of horror, no haunted atmosphere to cause shivers, no fairy spite, simply a troop of spirits, under human direction, bringing guilty minds into a state of repentance.

# The characters

**Prospero**

I find my zenith doth depend upon
A most auspicious star.

By the study of magic Prospero lost his dukedom; by the practical exercise of that magic he regained what he had lost and a happy marriage for his daughter into the bargain. The intervening twelve years he spent in educating Miranda and perfecting his plans in readiness for the day when fortune should bring his enemies into his power. In the space of three hours his triumph is complete.

Just as events are so subject to his control as to deprive the play of any dramatic suspense, so his personality dominates the stage to an extent that some have found unbearable. He speaks more than three times as many lines as any other character; their subject-matter consists in the main of his past history, his magic powers and the successive stages of his 'project'. He reproves, lectures, threatens with a dry severity that must be imputed to a long period of sway in which he had ruled over a child, a savage and troops of spirits. The other side of his character is seen, in glimpses, in his tenderness towards Miranda in her lovemaking, his regret at parting with Ariel and the cordiality with which he greets the forgiven king and his courtiers.

Prospero's character traits may for convenience, be summarized as follows:

**1** *As Duke of Milan (prior to the events of the play)*
Devotion to the study of the occult, which withdrew him from public life.
Trust in others, particularly his brother, whose betrayal of him accounts for Prospero's sternness in the play.
Popularity with his subjects, which necessitated his being abandoned at sea.

**2** *As Magician of the Island (more powerful than any duke)*
Control over the supernatural: his art raises a storm and preserves the ship and her crew; charms Miranda to sleep and Ferdinand from moving; opens the pine to free Ariel and afflicts Caliban with cramps; calls up spirits, whether goddesses or

hounds.

Affection: centred on his daughter, though he is also fond of Ariel.

Dignity and kindness: harsh and imperious when crossed, but gracious and hospitable when all lie finally at his mercy.

An exact mind, which issues detailed instructions and expects them to be carried out to the letter.

Patience in biding his time.

Zeal for teaching, perfected in Miranda, wasted on Caliban.

Readiness to praise: Ariel for his services, Gonzalo for his kindness.

Readiness to threaten: Ariel with an oak, Caliban with cramps, Ferdinand with torture.

Fondness for the dramatic: the banquet, the masque, the 'restoration' to their parents of Ferdinand and Miranda.

Interest in the effect of his 'art' on others: panic of the passengers (I, 2, 207–8), distraction of the three guilty men (V, 1, 7).

Delight in being a spectator: Miranda's love-making; Ariel's tantalizing of the courtiers.

Use of his magic powers as a means to an end: after his enemies have repented and restored his dukedom he renounces his spells.

Philosophy: the worth of true love, the sacredness of the marriage vow, and the transitoriness of this life.

Prospero is not perfect, otherwise he would not be human.

He has no sense of humour.

He is often abrupt and abusive in his speech.

He is rather vain about his 'art'.

He blames his brother's malice more than his own neglect of 'worldly ends'.

He fiercely resents the wrongs done him.

He lacks any sympathy for Caliban, is severe even to his daughter and is to Ferdinand at first 'compos'd of harshness'.

It matters little whether Prospero represents James I or Shakespeare himself, or whether he is a personification of human intellect or of old age (he is made to be older than his story would indicate); actually his character is objective enough, that of a wronged nobleman utilizing magic to inspire remorse in those who have done him wrong. With the surrender of his magic powers he grows in stature. He draws a veil over the past: 'Let us not burden our remembrances/With a heaviness that's gone.' He turns from spells to meditation; 'Every third thought shall be my grave', and takes the audience into his confidence.

## Miranda

No wonder, sir;
But certainly a maid.

Miranda is unique in that her father and Caliban are the only two beings she has known. This makes her portrayal a difficult task, but Shakespeare has, of course, succeeded in doing this. Miranda has the simplicity and directness of one who has had no share in the artificiality and hypocrisy of court life. She says what she thinks and feels. Her innocent admiration of the strangers may amuse a sophisticated audience:

How many goodly creatures are there here!
How beauteous mankind is! (V, 1, 182–3)

but when her first love prompts her to say, 'I am your wife if you will marry me', the audience is made conscious of something it has lost – or never known.

Miranda (the Admirable One) resembles Marina (the Sea-Born One) in *Pericles* and Perdita (the Lost One) in *The Winter's Tale*, not only in the significance of her name but in her unspoilt freshness and wistful loveliness.

Like Caliban, she is so accustomed to apparitions that she takes Ferdinand for a spirit; to the young prince, who had admired many court ladies only to find in each some defect to offset her good qualities, Miranda's sweetness and modesty make her seem at first a goddess. She is full of open-hearted sympathy: for the shipwrecked sailors; for her father's sufferings; and for the toiling Ferdinand; but Caliban fills her with repugnance.

With Miranda's betrothal to Ferdinand the new generation is brought in to redress the balance of the old. In the bright vision of youth the past is forgotten and the future is full of promise.

## Ferdinand

For your sake
Am I this patient log-man.

Shakespeare's problem was to make the son of Alonso worthy of Miranda. Alonso's part in the banishment of Prospero is therefore minimized, while the villainy is concentrated in Prospero's brother, Antonio.

Ferdinand is as handsome in appearance as Miranda is beautiful, and his rank as heir to Naples makes the match as desirable politically as it is perfect in itself. In some respects he is the male counterpart of Miranda, modest, impressionable and affectionate. He grieves for the father whom he believes to be drowned, is immediately susceptible to the captivating island airs and humbly accepts the punishment inflicted on him, regarding it as service done for her whom he at first took for 'the goddess/On whom these airs attend!'

Ferdinand has courage, striking out lustily for the shore, and attempting to resist the wand-waving magician with his sword. His period of testing satisfactorily concluded, it appears that he will become a dutiful son-in-law to his 'second father', as he forgets the gay and crowded life of Naples in the small but charmed circle of Prospero's cell. 'Let me live here ever;/So rare a wonder'd father and a wise/Makes this place Paradise.'

Prospero's own comment as he watches the young couple together expresses the sense of their fitness for each other that the playwright intended to convey: 'Fair encounter/Of two most rare affections!'

## Ariel

I drink the air before me.

No human actor can do more than approximate to the daintiness of Ariel. He trips across the stage, skips to Prospero's shoulder, and steals unseen to other human ears to whisper warning or defiance. His habitat is a flowering twig, his table a cowslip's bell, his chariot a bat's back. His movements are swift as lightning – he *is* lightning. His music (in stage properties, 'tabor and pipe') echoes through the island, haunting the ears and controlling the movements of his charges.

Ariel's attitude to Prospero is one of respect and dutiful obedience: 'What would my potent master? Here I am.' He performs all his tasks and reports on them, in detail, with a zest and a pride in his powers equal to the satisfaction with which Prospero displays his 'art'. Once, indeed, he proves petulant at the imposition of 'more toil' (surely an inappropriate term for one so obviously at home in the elements of sea, air and land), but his protest draws down such a lecture that he shows no further hesitation, though his programme proves to be a full one. He 'comes with a thought' and awaits his orders on tip-toe. His freedom is certainly well-earned:

Remember I have done thee worthy service;
Told thee no lies, made no mistakings, serv'd
Without or grudge or grumblings ... (I, 2, 247–9)

However much he longs to be free, he never stoops to treachery. A spirit less loyal than Ariel might have connived at Caliban's attempt to assassinate Prospero (unless, indeed, the spoken word of his master was necessary to break the spell). As it is, he reports the plan to Prospero, though so preoccupied is his master with the happiness of his daughter and the persecution of Alonso that the information would seem to have escaped his memory until it recurs to him rather suddenly towards the end of the masque.

It may be argued that Ariel's diligence is merely in his own interests; that, impatient of the yoke of a human intelligence employing him, and eager to recover his former irresponsible existence, he works only to one end – his liberty. This, however, is a narrow view; there is an unmistakable bond between spirit and magician, which is something more than a term of service. Prospero frequently uses terms of affection to Ariel; 'my dainty Ariel', 'my bird', 'tricksy spirit', 'fine apparition', and, as a last term of endearment, 'my Ariel, chick'. To Ariel, Prospero is 'noble master', 'grave sir', 'my commander'. The two are intimate partners in the work of enchantment, Prospero bringing to it the clear intention and moral purpose of a human mind, Ariel the swift and miraculous execution of an elemental spirit. The final triumph is shared between them alone:

*Ari.* Was't well done?
*Pro.* Bravely, my diligence. Thou shalt be free. (V, 1, 240–1)

Ariel, then, has a clearly defined character. It lacks two essentially human features: original thought, and depth of feeling. His speeches are a recital of his past performances. Only once, in giving Caliban the lie, does he indulge in a prank of his own. And when he describes the desperate state of the prisoners, he expresses a compassion for them that a spirit who is 'but air' cannot actually feel. He can only suggest that Prospero's heart would melt at the sight; as for his own 'affections': 'Mine would, sir, were I human.'

## Caliban

> I must eat my dinner.
> This island's mine...

In direct contrast to the dainty Ariel, moving with the speed of light, is the uncouth Caliban, crouching and cursing in his den.

The offspring of a witch, scraping a solitary living in the rocks, holes and trees of the island that then belonged to him, listening with animal fascination to its aerial music, gazing with uncomprehending awe at the sky overhead, and lacking ideas and the language with which to clothe them, Caliban at first welcomed the superior stranger who started with missionary zeal to educate him. Elevated from digging with his long nails for edible roots or snaring the smaller wild creatures to lessons in astronomy, and further won over by pats on the shoulder and sips of what appears to be coffee, he revealed to Prospero the island knowledge which he offers later on to Stephano.

> And then I lov'd thee
> And show'd thee all the qualities o' th' isle,
> The fresh springs, brine-pits, barren place and fertile ... (I, 2, 338–40)

After his brutish instincts had led him to offend against Miranda, the 'man-monster' was reduced by the indignant father to the servitude in which he appears at the beginning of the play. Hence Prospero's harsh intolerance of a creature more deserving of pity than of punishment; though here it must be pointed out that this last outstanding imaginative creation of Shakespeare is so vaguely delineated that one cannot be sure whether Caliban is a pitiful savage being mercilessly penalized or a dangerous monster who has to be kept in subjection by crippling his movements.

One thing is certain – we must not see Caliban through Prospero's eyes. He must have acquired from his former tutor a considerable vocabulary of abuse if the epithets hurled at him – 'poisonous slave', 'earth', 'filth', 'malice', 'tortoise', 'hag-seed', 'mis-shapen knave', 'thing of darkness', 'demi-devil' are any indication. The severity that mars the exiled Duke of Milan reaches its peak in his treatment of the dispossessed inhabitant of the island. Prospero's one subject gives him more trouble than the whole teeming population of a town once did.

The critic finds Caliban as much of a problem as he is to his tyrant of a master. He puzzles all who behold him for the first time, and their comments reveal only a misproportioned human being in a gaberdine and smelling strongly of fish.

Alonso, who has just seen and heard of some remarkable things, exclaims, 'This is a strange thing as e'er I look'd on.' Stephano and Trinculo immediately dub Caliban 'moon-calf', that is, an ignorant savage inhabiting these strange parts. They differ, however, in their attitude – Stephano well content with the monster's homage and pitying his 'ague', Trinculo scoffing at his simplicity in worshipping a drunken butler.

In these two rogues poor Caliban places his hopes of a speedy end to his present slavery – by changing one master for another, the cunning sorcerer for the man in the moon with his 'celestial liquor'. Better to be Stephano's 'boot-licker' than the slave of Prospero.

Caliban explains carefully how to kill the sleeping magician, only to see his plans go astray as 'king' and 'viceroy' squabble over the 'frippery'. So great is his fear of Prospero that he does not carry the knife himself. When, however, he has seen Stephano and Trinculo ignominiously chased by dogs, he realizes his error and, with the promise of pardon (instead of the threat of pinches) ringing in his ears, hastens to perform the last of his household offices.

It might be claimed for Caliban that he is as indispensable to *The Tempest* as Falstaff is to *Henry IV*. Both are gross, sensual and cowardly, nursing grudges and cursing roundly, yet possessing a native shrewdness, a species of low cunning, and at the same time a relish for things fine and fair. The contrast between what they are and what they would be arouses much-needed laughter.

Both are original creations, bold caricatures with sources of inspiration that can only be guessed at. While Prince Hal's 'old lad of the castle' provides a clue to the identity of Falstaff, hints in our play have suggested three plausible explanations of Caliban. His nature-worship and fondness for 'fire-water' are characteristic of the American Indian, made landless by the colonist; his odour and deformity place him in the category of the sea-monster at the fair; and his torments and curses give him an affinity to the native African toiling in the settlements. His name is probably an anagram of 'cannibal'.

Whatever he may be intended to represent, the reader will not have overlooked Caliban's habit of speaking in verse, in contrast to the prose used by his comrades and employed by Shakespeare for less dignified utterances. This is in keeping with the sensitiveness to beauty that lies beneath his ugly exterior. He exalts Miranda above his own mother, admires the restored Duke in his fine clothes, and, in describing the music that haunts his dreams, even breaks out into a vein of poetry.

*Character contrast of Ariel and Caliban*

| Ariel | Caliban |
| --- | --- |
| Spirit of air | Creature of earth |
| Soulless being | A soul in darkness |
| Speedy and dainty | Clumsy and uncouth |
| Associated with bees and flowers | Associated with adders and hedgehogs |
| Desires freedom | Desires vengeance |
| Serves Prospero willingly | Serves Prospero reluctantly |
| Raises a storm at sea | Does menial services |
| Casts spells | Is tormented by cramps |

**Alonso, Antonio, Sebastian**

> You three
> From Milan did supplant good Prospero.

For the sake of his son Ferdinand, Alonso's character is made far less black than that of Antonio. In fact, his part is one of sorrow, amazement and repentance. However, the banishment of Prospero was a cruel crime, and Alonso suffers for it. While Prospero emphasizes to Miranda the guilt of his brother, it is Alonso, 'an enemy to me inveterate', who endures the worst punishment of the 'three men of sin'.

The other two, considering their share in the banishment, their despicable behaviour and heartless levity throughout the play, and their treasonable attempt on the King's life, escape with only an hour of frenzied despair and a secret reprimand. They never show any sign of repentance for the wrongs they have done or thankfulness for their preservation. It is not the first time in Shakespeare that, for the sake of a happy ending, such unworthy characters are treated better than they deserve.

Antonio is completely cynical. His conscience is a 'kibe', Gonzalo an 'ancient morsel', Alonso 'no better than the earth he lies upon', and the rest of the court (who, indeed, have little to say for themselves) will be only too ready to accept a *fait accompli*.

Actually, it is Sebastian who 'takes suggestion as a cat laps milk', but his slow (or cautious) perception of Antonio's meaning serves to create an appreciable period of suspense for the audience. Previously, he has been the one to throw the blame on his brother for the general misfortune (II, 1); now he makes his resolve only when he has seen a 'precedent' in Antonio's treatment of Prospero. Thus this other 'unnatural brother' is more of an accomplice of the chief villain; he would gain a throne by the death of Alonso, but there is a motive in Antonio's proposition, duly recognized by his partner:

> one stroke
> Shall free thee from the tribute that thou payest.

As it would be 'unnatural' for Sebastian to kill his brother, this was to be Antonio's task, thereby earning for him the independence of Milan.

## Gonzalo

> My true preserver, and a loyal sir
> To him thou follow'st!

When we hear that Gonzalo's 'tears run down his beard', we wonder why the old man should have to share the punishment of the others. This incongruity, however, is soon forgotten when we see Prospero for the only time show outward signs of emotion, out of sympathy for the man who was responsible for his own preservation.

The old courtier, indeed, has a character of his own – a compound of Adam, the faithful retainer in *As You Like It*, and Polonius, the garrulous old counsellor in *Hamlet*. His remarks provide a 'chorus' (in the dramatic sense) to each successive incident of the main plot. He is most anxious to cheer the despondent King and to save him from himself when demented with sorrow. The well-meaning, however, sometimes exceed the patience of those they seek to comfort, and Gonzalo sees it as his duty to keep on talking, when all Alonso needs is rest and quiet.

Gonzalo is not easily discouraged. He first places the hopes of all on the boatswain's destiny and is delighted to find his prophecy come true, though in strange manner. After praying for 'an acre of barren ground' when last seen clinging to the wreckage, he is charmed with the prospect of the island on which he has miraculously set foot and creates for it an ideal commonwealth. Soon, however, he is to be alarmed by the thought of wild beasts and fatigued by 'forth-rights and meanders'. His spirits revive sufficiently for him to admire the music of the place and to chuckle over the travellers' tales he will tell in Naples of the monstrous though gentle inhabitants. Then, after Prospero's charm has tormented the three guilty ones, he finds it no place for an Utopia:

All torment, trouble, wonder and amazement
Inhabits here; some heavenly power guide us
Out of this fearful country! (V, 1, 104–6)

Finally, the apparition of the Duke whom he last saw off in a leaky hulk twelve years before deprives him temporarily of speech, until, perceiving the hand of Fate in this happy ending, he piously calls down a blessing on the young couple.

### Stephano and Trinculo

It is fitting, in this last play of Shakespeare, that there should appear a drunken echo of Sir John Falstaff and Sir Toby Belch, together with a rather feeble flicker of the clown's wit that sparkles through his comedies. There is a difference here, in that it is the clown who also gets drunk and the drunkard who also sings.

At their first sight of Caliban's gaberdine, each thinks of a natural monster who will make a fortune for him at home in Naples. When Caliban proves to be something a little higher, he is welcomed as a subject by Stephano, but turned into a butt by Trinculo – who also holds aloof when Caliban's knowledge of the island raises him to a share in Stephano's plans. Trinculo pays for his mockery of the 'moon-calf' after Ariel has taken a hand in the discussion; it is now Caliban's turn to laugh at the discomfited clown. After he has been struck, Trinculo is content to play 'viceroy' in the new regime about to be set up on the island.

Once Stephano and Trinculo have been assured by Caliban that the invisible musician is there not to terrify, but to entertain them, they are once more united in their work of possessing themselves of the island. They follow the irresistible music and experience such mishaps as can only be related by Ariel, not performed on the stage. When they appear again, they have lost their bottle in the pool and are incensed with Caliban over the tricks played by his 'harmless fairy'. Their troubles are not over; ignoring his warning against pilfering gown and jerkin, they are chased by hounds and pinched by goblins. Finally, they are driven by Ariel into their master's presence, in such a pickle as to provide a last touch of comic relief at the close of the play.

# Style

## Introduction

The vocabulary of Shakespeare's works has been calculated to exceed fifteen thousand different words, well ahead of his nearest competitor John Milton, with eight thousand. They include many which, once in everyday Elizabethan use, are now obsolete, e.g. 'mow' (make faces), and others whose meanings have changed, e.g. 'stomach' (courage). Shakespeare must have been an omnivorous reader, with a comprehensive memory. Such a well-stocked mind, combined with great imaginative powers, enabled him not only to compose the dialogue of lifelike characters, but also create the background and the atmosphere in which they moved.

His earliest manner was often daringly experimental, trying out far-fetched analogies and intricate figures of speech; his 'middle period', as it has been called, struck a more even balance between idea and expression; in his great tragedies strong emotions and a wealth of imagery break the restraints of precise grammar, plain logic and metrical regularity to reach an eloquence beyond what had gone before and rarely been equalled since; in the final 'romantic' comedies, after a lifetime of poetic invention, there is often a crowding together of ideas, greater freedom and looser sentence structure, with frequent elision. In *The Tempest* this development is less noticeable, as the action is too simple and rapid for close-packed metaphors. The longer speeches are mostly taken up with descriptions of present or past events, and the diction is rarely too extravagant for ready comprehension. Where there is obscurity it is due to condensation, especially in the utterances of the terse and abrupt Prospero. Epigrams are few:

> the rarer action
> Is in virtue than in vengeance (V,1,27–8)

The natural setting of the island supplies some of the imagery: 'the still-closing waters' (III,3,64), 'ebbing men' (II,1,221), 'the approaching tide/Will shortly fill the reasonable shore' (V,1,80–81). There are half a dozen words compounded with 'sea', none of which is found elsewhere in Shakespeare: 'sea-storm' and 'sea-sorrow' in Prospero's talk with Miranda, 'sea-swallow'd' in Antonio's urging of Sebastian, 'sea-marge' in the stilted lines of the masque, and the immortal 'sea-change' and 'Sea-nymphs' in Ariel's song to Ferdinand.

Inversions are frequent – (1) object preceding verb (I, 2, 225):

The mariners, say how thou hast dispos'd

In I, 2, 494–6 there are two in quick succession:

> all corners else o' th' earth
> Let liberty make use of; space enough
> Have I in such a prison.

Gonzalo has a multiple example in II,1,156–8. The emphatic nature of inversion is seen in that of the complement in III,1,92:

So glad of this as they I cannot be

Inversion is, of course, frequent in rhymed verse (IV, 1, 84):

A contract of true love to celebrate

(2) verb preceding subject, often resulting in Elizabethan speech in a singular verb introducing a plural subject (IV,1,263):

Lies at my mercy all mine enemies

See also I,1,16; I,2,481; and V,1,7.

The use in the play of the familiar second singular pronoun 'thou' is not consistent, but note how Ariel's affectionate address to his master in I,2 changes to a taciturn 'ay, sir' and 'no, sir' after the rebuke over a suggested reduction in working hours. Caliban says 'thou' to Prospero when speaking of their earlier relationship, then 'you' when cursing the severe regime which followed. The tender regard of Ferdinand and Miranda for each other is expressed by 'you' throughout, even over the chessboard!

The looser grammar of those days is reflected in such offences to modern ears as 'thou did' and 'thou was'.

## Verse

*Metre* defines the rhythm of each line of verse by the number and nature of its 'feet': (1) iambic (scanned ×/), two syllables with the stress on the second; (2) trochaic (/×), two syllables with the stress on the first; (3) anapaestic (××/), three syllables with the stress on the last; (4) dactylic (/××), three syllables with the stress on the first. The bulk of English verse and of Shakespeare's dramatic dialogue is in 'verses' of five feet (×/), called 'iambic pentameters'; where these are unrhymed they constitute 'blank verse':

Ĭ háve wĭth súch prŏvísiŏn ín mĭne Árt

A 'verse', now employed of a group of lines, was originally a single line which was 'turned' (versus) at a particular point for the beginning of another line.

*Rhyme* (strictly 'rime', misspelt through confusion with 'rhythm') is the agreement (sometimes approximate) in sound of the final syllables of two or more lines. Much of Shakespeare's early work is in rhymed (heroic) couplets; later these were used mainly as a sign of the end of a scene (II, 1):

Prospero my lord shall know what I have done:
So, King, go safely on to seek thy son.

This metre suits the conventional and artificial dialogue of the masque in IV,1. The stanzas of the more attractive song by Juno and Ceres are trochaic lines of seven or eight syllables (octosyllabic), arranged in quatrains. The lilting effect of trochaic verse is at its best in the lovely lyrics of Ariel, respectively a dance, a lament, a warning, and a paean of joy. The pace quickens in the last two lines of the fourth into the only example of the dactylic:

Merrily, merrily shall I live now
Under the blossom that hangs on the bough.

The Epilogue is in octosyllabic couplets, alternating irregularly between iambic and trochaic.

## Use of prose

Pentameters being the normal form of Shakespeare's dialogue, prose is used for special purposes:
1 Where intellectual argument rather than emotional expression is concerned; prose is the vehicle for witty repartees, verse for poetic imagery. Clowns use prose.
2 Where ordinary citizens are involved in everyday affairs, lacking historic or tragic importance (*The Merry Wives of Windsor* is mostly in prose). Verse is for the aristocracy.

**3** For comic characters, like Falstaff, Bottom or Stephano. Caliban is not a comic, but a deprived soul in a disadvantaged body, hence his verse outpourings.

Some of Shakespeare's best-known characters speak now in verse, now in prose, according to the mood of the moment or the spirit of the occasion. Prospero never deviates into prose; doubtless the saga of his exile, narrated in epic-style pentameters, would help the evening 'go quick away'.

# General questions plus questions on related topics for coursework/examinations on other books you may be studying

**1 Indicate (1) similarities, and (2) differences between the two conspiracies, showing also how each was frustrated.**

*Suggested notes for essay answer*:

(1) Both to be attempted while victims were asleep – for possession of territory and title of 'King' – blow to be given by proxy, Antonio for Sebastian, Stephano for Caliban (the real organiser) – both foreseen by Prospero and prevented by Ariel on his instructions (whereas the sprite is allowed a freer hand with his baiting of Trinculo and Caliban) – in both cases the conspirators believe they will meet with no resistance.

(2) Antonio and Sebastian are greedy for power, Caliban longs for freedom (he seems to have no knowledge of Ariel, whereas the guilty men are confronted by a harpy) – considerable suspense is built up by Antonio's lengthy persuasion of Sebastian, who is then determined to act; Stephano jumps at the idea, but is later easily decoyed from carrying it out. One set of conspirators is dead drunk, the other in deadly earnest. The ridiculous is the comic counterpart of the sinister: any blunt instrument or kitchen-knife as against the sword. Thwarting: Ariel's alerting of Gonzalo; later the fear inspired by the apparitions. The two traitors are secretly warned, without punishment and without forgiveness, which is reserved for their intended victim (whose crime belongs to the remote past). For the drunken trio there is no forgiveness for something they were incapable (through alcohol or magic) of committing; only abrupt dismissal to domestic chores.

**2** Give an uninterrupted version of the discourse with which Gonzalo attempts to console Alonso. Is the King's rebuke justified?

**3**
> 'This must crave
> An if this be at all, a most strange story.'

Describe and explain the wonders that are yet to amaze Alonso.

**4** The different groups meet only in the final scene. List and account for the various surprises encountered.

**5** What dramatic purposes are served by (a) the dumb-show, (b) the masque? How far do you find them appropriate?

**6** Discuss Shakespeare's use of the supernatural in *The Tempest*.

**7** Compare the situation and abilities of Trinculo with those of any two other professional clowns in Shakespeare.

**8** Examine Prospero's character and his dealings with others under the three aspects of duke, magician and father.

**9** Would you interpret Prospero's farewell speeches as masking Shakespeare's own feelings at the end of his career?

**10** Ariel's character is the only one to emerge from the island's spirit population; how does it compare with those in the other fairy-play, *A Midsummer Night's Dream*?

**11** How many different kinds of music are employed in the play? Suggest suitable instruments to produce the various effects.

**12** What hints, if any, do you think Shakespeare drops on the subject of (a) the discharge of political duties, (b) the treatment of primitive peoples, (c) the usefulness of hard work?

**13** Does forgiveness make as dramatic an end to a play as any other? How far do you consider Prospero's attitude part of a diplomatic scheme to unite Milan with Naples?

**14** Suggest alternative titles to the play. Can you justify any of them as more suitable?

**15** Contrast, quoting as fully as you can, the characters of Ariel and Caliban.

**16** Which pair of lovers in Shakespeare comes nearest to Ferdinand and Miranda? In what respects do they differ?

**17** Find two other Shakespeare plays whose opening scenes are in your opinion as dramatic as the shipwreck, and justify your choice.

**18** Supposing the extant version of the play to represent a shortened form of the original, supply in outline the missing scenes.

**19** Make as complete a list as you can of stage properties, other than costumes and musical instruments, required for a performance of the play, mentioning the context of each.

**20** In any of your books, give an account of a setting or location where most of the action occurs.

**21** Indicate the effect of the supernatural or magical in any book you have studied.

**22** Write about a character who appears to be primitive or uncivilized in his or her attitudes.

**23** Describe the theme of forgiveness or reconciliation in a book you have read recently.

**24** Write an account of a romance between two young lovers in one of your books.

**25** Describe a character in a book you have read who, you feel, has dominated the action of the story.

**26** Explain how good triumphs over evil either in a play you have seen or a story you have read.

**27** Write about a novel or play where a group of characters contribute to the humour of the story.

**28** Compare and contrast any *two* characters in a book you have read.

**29** Relate the plot of a book where you feel that the ending is either completely convincing or very improbable, and say why.

# Further reading

The number of books on Shakespeare and especially a play as popular as *The Tempest* is very great. The student is recommended to consult:

*The Arden Shakespeare: The Tempest*, edited by Frank Kermode (Methuen, 1954)

*A Shakespeare Encyclopaedia*, ed. Campbell and Quinn (Methuen 1966).

*William Shakespeare*, E. K. Chambers (OUP 1930).

*Shakespeare and his World*, F. E. Halliday (Thames and Hudson 1956).

*Everyman's Companion to Shakespeare*, G. & B. Lloyd Evans (Dent 1978)

*Shakespeare: English Men of Letters*, Sir Walter Raleigh (Macmillan)

Any large central library will have (for reference) a copy in reduced facsimile of the First Folio.

# Brodie's Notes

## TITLES IN THE SERIES

| | |
|---|---|
| Jane Austen | Pride and Prejudice |
| Robert Bolt | A Man for All Seasons |
| Emily Brontë | Wuthering Heights |
| Charlotte Brontë | Jane Eyre |
| Geoffrey Chaucer | Prologue to the Canterbury Tales |
| Geoffrey Chaucer | The Nun's Priest's Tale |
| Geoffrey Chaucer | The Wife of Bath's Tale |
| Geoffrey Chaucer | The Pardoner's Prologue and Tale |
| Charles Dickens | Great Expectations |
| Gerald Durrell | My Family and Other Animals |
| T. S. Eliot | Selected Poems |
| George Eliot | Silas Marner |
| F. Scott Fitzgerald | The Great Gatsby and Tender is the Night |
| E. M. Forster | A Passage to India |
| John Fowles | The French Lieutenant's Woman |
| Anne Frank | The Diary of Anne Frank |
| William Golding | Lord of the Flies |
| Graham Handley (ed) | The Metaphysical Poets: John Donne to Henry Vaughan |
| Thomas Hardy | Far From the Madding Crowd |
| Thomas Hardy | Tess of the D'Urbervilles |
| Thomas Hardy | The Mayor of Casterbridge |
| Aldous Huxley | Brave New World |
| John Keats | Selected Poems and Letters of John Keats |
| Philip Larkin | Selected Poems of Philip Larkin |
| D. H. Lawrence | Sons and Lovers |
| Laurie Lee | Cider with Rosie |
| Harper Lee | To Kill a Mockingbird |
| Arthur Miller | The Crucible |
| Arthur Miller | Death of a Salesman |
| George Orwell | 1984 |
| George Orwell | Animal Farm |
| J. B. Priestley | An Inspector Calls |
| J. D. Salinger | The Catcher in the Rye |
| William Shakespeare | The Merchant of Venice |
| William Shakespeare | King Lear |
| William Shakespeare | A Midsummer Night's Dream |
| William Shakespeare | Twelfth Night |
| William Shakespeare | Hamlet |
| William Shakespeare | As You Like It |
| William Shakespeare | Romeo and Juliet |
| William Shakespeare | Julius Caesar |
| William Shakespeare | Macbeth |
| William Shakespeare | Antony and Cleopatra |
| William Shakespeare | Othello |
| William Shakespeare | The Tempest |

| | |
|---|---|
| George Bernard Shaw | Pygmalion |
| Alan Sillitoe | Selected Fiction |
| John Steinbeck | Of Mice and Men and The Pearl |
| Alice Walker | The Color Purple |

ENGLISH COURSEWORK BOOKS

| | |
|---|---|
| Terri Apter | Women and Society |
| Kevin Dowling | Drama and Poetry |
| Philip Gooden | Conflict |
| Philip Gooden | Science Fiction |
| Margaret K. Gray | Modern Drama |
| Graham Handley | Modern Poetry |
| Graham Handley | Prose |
| Graham Handley | Childhood and Adolescence |
| R. J. Sims | The Short Story |